A.L.A. GLOSSARY OF

Library Terms

WITH A SELECTION OF TERMS IN RELATED FIELDS

Prepared under the Direction of the
Committee on Library Terminology
of the American Library Association
by

ELIZABETH H. THOMPSON

AMERICAN LIBRARY ASSOCIATION
CHICAGO, ILLINOIS, 1943

Tenth Printing, 1968

COPYRIGHT 1943 BY THE AMERICAN LIBRARY ASSOCIATION

Manufactured in the United States of America

PREFACE

THE NEED OF A MORE COMPREHENSIVE COLLECTION OF DEFINITIONS OF LIBRARY terms than any in print was felt so keenly by the Board of Education for Librarianship of the American Library Association that in 1926 definite plans were made to meet the need. Elizabeth M. Smith, a member of the Board, was put in charge of the new project and her report, *Standard Terminology in Education with Particular Reference to Librarianship,* was issued by the Board in mimeographed form in 1927. The Board continued to show its interest in library terminology by appointing a committee in 1929 with Jennie M. Flexner, a member, as chairman to carry forward Miss Smith's work. This committee asked for volunteer readers to search library literature for terms and definitions of interest to American librarians. Approximately one thousand terms, including those on Miss Smith's list, were collected.

Many of the problems involved in this work became apparent during the succeding two years. At the request of the Board of Education for Librarianship in 1931 the Executive Board of the American Library Association created a separate committee to make a study of terminology and appointed Susan Grey Akers as its chairman. With the terms and definitions previously collected as a basis for its work the Committee on Library Terminology studied the problem and considered the possibility of preparing a glossary.

Following the method of the preceding committee a call was made for volunteer readers to continue the work of gathering terms and definitions. This request met a ready response. Two hundred and fifty librarians from British Columbia to Florida offered their services and read a great number of volumes during 1934-1936.

In 1935 the Committee made a formal report of its work. A recommendation was made that a glossary be published, and funds were requested to carry out this recommendation. In January, 1937, the Carnegie Corporation of New York through a generous grant supplied the funds that made possible the preparation of this glossary.

Another call for assistance in 1937 received the same response as that accorded the earlier request. Librarians, far too many for individual acknowledgments here, gave generously of their time in advising the Committee on their choice of terms for inclusion in the glossary. When it became apparent that the original plan to issue a preliminary edition for critical purposes would not be feasible, it was decided to publish one edition leaving revision and perfecting to the future. The Committee decided to work directly through a full-time editor, cooperating with other A.L.A. committees at work upon similar projects and with individual authorities in the various fields of library interest.

Dr. Lulu Ruth Reed, a graduate of the University of Chicago Library School, was chosen editor. She began work upon the glossary in August, 1938, and did a very good piece of work in organizing the material. Work on the actual preparation of definitions had begun when she found it necessary to resign in the spring of 1939. In September, 1939, Miss Elizabeth H. Thompson, Head of the Catalog Department of the University of North Carolina, accepted the editorship on a part-time basis, and has been employed for several different periods. Unanticipated circumstances postponed the final work upon the glossary until the spring of 1942.

The preparation of the glossary has been a cooperative enterprise, with many librarians participating in the work. To them collectively the Committee wishes to acknowledge its indebtedness. For the assistance given by the Subcommitee on Definitions of the A.L.A. Catalog Code Revision Committee, other organized groups, and many individuals in permitting the use of material gathered and prepared by them and for their advice, the Committee is particularly grateful.

In addition to the present members the following have served at various times upon the A.L.A. Committee on Library Terminology: Esther Betz, Julia E. Elliott, Ralph E. Ellsworth, Helen E. Farr, Frances A. Hannum, Elizabeth MacBride King, Jesse Lee Rader, Flora B. Roberts, Martha Rosentreter, and Ralph R. Shaw.

In June, 1941, the Committee became the Subcommittee on Library Terminology of the A.L.A. Editorial Committee.

GEORGIA H. FAISON *(Chairman, 1936-1938)*
JENNIE M. FLEXNEF
LODA MAY HOPKINS
M. LOUISE HUNT
AMY C. MOON
LINDA H. MORLEY
MARIAN SHAW
JESSE H. SHERA
SUSAN GREY AKERS, *Chairman.*

INTRODUCTION

THIS GLOSSARY OF LIBRARY AND RELATED TERMS WILL, IT IS HOPED, PROVE to be of value to librarians in their work, to library school students, and perhaps, occasionally, to others outside the library profession.

The glossary includes technical terms used in American libraries, except those purely, or largely, of local significance; some terms not in current use but of historical interest; and selected terms in several fields more or less closely related to library work, with which librarians come in contact in connection with books and the history of books, as, archives, bibliography, printing and publishing, paper, binding, illustration and prints. A few types of material used in libraries—certain kinds of reference books, for instance—have been selected for inclusion. Foreign terms, with a few exceptions have been omitted.

In this attempt to collect and formulate definitions for a profession composed of varied elements, much assistance has been received from many librarians.

Definitions of catalog and bibliography terms in the preliminary American second edition of the *A.L.A. Catalog Rules* have been reprinted in the glossary with as little change as possible on their removal from their setting as part of a code. This cooperation was planned in order that the publications might be used interchangeably for definitions of these terms.

Other terms in bibliography have been included to some extent, with definitions prepared by librarians interested in bibliography. Terms distinguishing the various kinds of bibliography that have been the subject of discussion by bibliographers, as historical, anatomical, enumerative, etc., have been omitted. Excellent discussions may be found in W. W. Greg's "What is Bibliography?" (*Transactions* of the Bibliographical Society, London, v.12 (1914) p.39-53), G. W. Cole's "Bibliography—a Forecast" (in *Papers* of the Bibliographical Society of America, v.14 (1920) p.1-19), and H. B. Van Hoesen and F. K. Walter's *Bibliography, Practical, Enumerative, Historical*.

Although archives are sometimes housed in libraries, archives administration, differs from library administration, and a separate vocabulary has developed. It was hoped that a considerable number of terms from this field might be included, but, as archivists are not fully agreed on the meanings of these terms, the choice has been limited to a few of the most commonly used terms.

Definitions for bookbinding terms have been taken, with some slight changes, from definitions prepared by Louis N. Feipel for a projected manual on binding. Music terms have been limited to those connected with the technique of cataloging, and definitions have been based upon material in the *A.L.A. Catalog Rules* and the preliminary draft of a general handbook on cataloging and the care of music in course of preparation by the Music Library Association. Terms relating to musical composition have not been included. The few terms relating to maps are those used in handling a general map collection and a few connected with the cataloging of old maps. Groups of terms omitted are those for paper sizes, book sizes (with the exception of a few of the more commonly used terms), and names of the various styles and sizes of type.

In view of the present tendency to substitute modern uniform terms for the older terms indicating character of the work performed, the Committee hoped to include in the appendix a list of the various personnel terms in use in different types of libraries. This plan was given up when the number of terms became very extensive and no uniformity was discernible. The more stabilized terms have been defined.

Appendixes give tables of book and type sizes, and a list of abbreviations, collected as a by-product of the work of gathering terms, and not intended to be exhaustive.

The arrangement of the glossary is alphabetical, each term having a separate entry; there is no arrangement by subject. The terms are not articulated by a system of "see also" references, but synonymous terms are generally given with the definitions and "see" references from synonymous terms are numerous. Definitions from the *A.L.A. Catalog Rules* are indicated by C and Ca (if definition is altered) following the definitions. Terms in microphotography are indicated by M, since most of these terms are very technical and appear unrelated to the terminology for printed and manuscript materials with which librarians are more familiar. A few definitions have been reprinted from copyrighted material in dictionaries, as noted after the definitions quoted.

The editor wishes to acknowledge her obligations to the Catalog Code Revision Committee for the privilege of using definitions from the *A.L.A. Catalog Rules;* the group of members of the Special Libraries Association, under the direction of Linda M. Morley, for the contribution of many definitions in the special libraries field; the A.L.A. Committee on Photographic Reproduction of Library Materials, which, through F. G. Kilgour, prepared definitions for microphotography terms; the Music Library Association for the use of several definitions taken from the preliminary version of its *Code for Cataloging Music*; Louis N. Feipel, whose fund of definitions of binding terms has been used freely; R. W. Henderson for advice about definitions for certain terms relating to book stacks; Solon J. Buck for preparing definitions of terms used in archives administration; Frank K. Walter for advice in formulating definitions of printing terms; Frank Weitenkampf for criticism and help in defining illustrations and prints; Lucy E. Goldthwaite and Mrs. Fannie R. Howley for assistance in preparing definitions of terms used in libraries for the blind; William A. Jackson, who as a representative of the Bibliographical Society of America, made suggestions about definitions for some of the terms in bibliography, though he is not at all responsible for their final form; Harriet D. MacPherson and Eunice Lathrope for criticism and suggestions regarding certain bibliography terms; Mrs. Clara N. de Villa for reviewing alterations of definitions from *A.L.A. Catalog Rules* and offering most helpful advice about definitions for related terms; and other individuals who have criticized or have written definitions of single terms or groups of terms. The editor owes special gratitude to the chairman of the Committee, who has watched over the development of the glossary from its beginning and is particularly responsible for its materialization; and to Georgia H. Faison, Chapel Hill member of the Committee, whose constant advice and many hours of practical work over a long period have been of inestimable value.

Many books and articles have been used in the search for definition material, and while acknowledgement is made to individual authors and publishers for the privilege of reprinting copyrighted material, acknowledgement is also due to many unnamed sources that suggested definitions. Cutter's *Rules for a Dictionary Catalog*, often used as a source for definitions in cataloging, has furnished material also for the glossary; and material in A.L.A. publications has been drawn upon freely.

Acknowledgements for the privilege of reprinting certain definitions are offered to the following authors and publishers: J. Christian Bay, *The Fortune of Books*, c1941 by the author (Chicago, Walter M. Hill) (library science); Lloyd A. Brown, *Notes on the Care & Cataloguing of Old Maps*, c1940 by the author (Windham, Connecticut, Hawthorn House) (edition (old maps), issue (old maps)); The University of Chicago Press, *A Manual of Style*, 10th ed., c1937 (book paper, body type, dummy); The F. W. Faxon Co., *A Glossary of Library Terms, English, Danish, Dutch, French, German, Italian, Spanish*, by A. F. C. M. Moth, c1915 by the Boston Book Co. (pamphlet volume); The Gilmary Society, *The Catholic Encyclopedia Dictionary*, c1941 (Index Librorum Prohibitorum); Harvard University Press, "Elizabethan Americana," by George Watson Cole, in *Bibliographical Essays, a Tribute to Wilberforce Eames*, 1924 (lost book, def. 1); Theresa Hitchler, *Cataloging for Small Libraries*, 3d ed., c1926 by the author (New York, G. E. Stechert & Co. (library economy); The Henry E. Huntington Library and Art Gallery, *Incunabula in the Huntington Library*, compiled by H. R. Mead, c1937 (Proctor order); *The Library*, " 'Facsimile' Reprints of Old Books," by A. W. Pollard (in 4th series, v.6, 1926) (period printing); Library Bureau Division of Remington Rand, Inc., definitions from Alice B. Kroeger's "Glossary of Library Terms," (in *Public Libraries*, v.1); J. J. Little and Ives Co., *The J. J. Little Book of Types, Specimen Pages and Book Papers, with Suggestions on Book Making and a Glossary of Printing and Binding Terms*, c1923 (offset, def. 1); New York Public Library, *Subscription Books*, by F. E. Compton, 1939 (subscription book); Oxford University Press, *Introduction to Bibliography for Literary Students*, by R. B. McKerrow, 1927, (collation [by signature]); Porte Publishing Co., Salt Lake City, Utah, *Dictionary of Printing Terms*, 4th ed., c1941 (text, def. 4); The Society of Motion Picture Engineers, *Journal*, v.17, November, 1931 (fixing, focal point, focus); Philip Van Doren Stern, *Introduction to Typography*, c1932 by the author (New York, Harper & Brothers) (cut).

ELIZABETH H. THOMPSON, *Editor*

Chapel Hill, N.C.
June, 1943

GLOSSARY

Abbreviated Catalog Card. A catalog card giving less information than the main entry.

Abridged Edition. *See* Abridgment.

Abridgment. A reduced form of a work produced by condensation and omission of more or less of detail, but retaining the general sense and unity of the original. [By permission; from Webster's *New International Dictionary,* Second Edition, copyright, 1934, 1939, by G. & C. Merriam Co.]

Absolute Location. *See* Fixed Location.

Absolute Size. *See* Exact Size.

Abstract. A brief summary that gives the essential points of a book, pamphlet, or article.

Abstract Bulletin. A printed or mimeographed bulletin containing abstracts of currently published periodical articles, pamphlets, etc., issued by a special library and distributed monthly, weekly, or daily to its clientele.

Abstract Journal or Periodical. A periodical consisting of abstracts of current material in books, pamphlets, and periodicals.

Abstracting Service. Abstracts in a particular field or on a particular subject prepared by an individual or a company and supplied regularly to subscribers or on request.

Academic Dissertation. *See* Dissertation, Academic.

Academy Publication. A work issued by an academy. Sometimes, in an inclusive sense, a work issued by any learned society.

Access to Shelves. *See* Open Shelves.

Accession. (*n.*) A book or other similar material acquired by a library for its collections. (*v.*) To record books and other similar material added to a library in the order of acquisition.

Accession Arrangement. An obsolete method of arranging books on the shelves in the order in which they were acquired.

Accession Date. The date on which a volume is entered in the accession record.

Accession Division. The section of an acquisition department that records, in chronological order of receipt, publications secured by purchase, exchange, or gift.

Accession Number. The number given to a volume in the order of its acquisition.

Accession Record. A record of the volumes added to a library in the order in which they are received. It may be known, from its various forms, as Accession Book, Accession Cards, Accession Catalog, Accession File, Accession Sheets, etc.

Accounts and Papers. A group of official British documents published in Parliamentary Papers, exclusive of Public Bills, Reports of Committees, and Reports of Commissioners.

Accredited Library School. A school offering education in librarianship that has been approved by the Board of Education for Librarianship of the American Library Association as meeting requirements adopted by the American Library Association Council for various types of library schools.

Acetate Film. *See* Cellulose Acetate. [M.]

Acquisition Department. The administrative unit in charge of selecting and acquiring books, periodicals, and other material by purchase, exchange, and gift, and of keeping the necessary records of these additions. Sometimes referred to as Order Department or Accession Department.

Acting Edition. An edition of a play that gives the text as used in stage production, often in a particular production, with entrances and exits, and other stage business.

Ad Interim Copyright. A temporary American copyright for a book in the English language published abroad, that may be extended to full copyright on fulfillment of certain requirements.

Adaptation. 1. A rewritten form of a literary work modified for a purpose or use other than that for which the original work was intended. 2. A new version based upon one or more versions of a given work or story. 3. Loosely, a free translation.

Added Copy. A duplicate of a book already in a library, if it is added, or to be added, to the library. Sometimes called Duplicate, and several added copies may be known as Multiple Copies.

Added Edition. An edition of a work acquired by a library that differs from editions already in the library.

Added Entry. In cataloging, a secondary entry, *i.e.*, any other than the main entry. *Cf.* Main Entry. There may be added entries for editor, translator, title, subjects, series, etc. [Ca.]
Some catalogers would restrict the use of the term added entry to any entry other than the main entry and subject entries, using secondary entry as a group term to include all entries other than the main entry. Others would make the opposite choice, using added entry as the group term to include secondary entry and subject entry. [Ca.]

Added Title Page. A title page complementary to the one chosen for the main entry of a work. The added title page may precede or follow the main title page with which it is issued and may be more general, as a series title page, or equally general, as a title page in another language either at the beginning or at the end of the work. [C.]

Addenda. Material essential to the completeness of the text of a book but less extensive than a supplement, usually added at the back of the book.

Adjustable Classification. A classification scheme designed by James Duff Brown for smaller English libraries, with a notation of letters and numbers allowing for later insertions.

Adjustable Shelf. A shelf the position of which may be easily changed to accommodate books of varying heights.

Admission Record. A permit, pass, attendance slip, or other form, used to check a student's attendance in a school library with his classroom and study hall schedules. Also called Admission Slip, Library Pass, Library Permit, and Permit.

Admission Slip. *See* Admission Record.

Adult Education. The acquisition of knowledge by those beyond school age, obtained through such agencies as continuation and vocational schools, folk schools and workers' schools, classes for illiterates, lectures, forums, directed reading, library service, and the radio.

Advance Copy. A copy of a book sent out before publication date for review, notice, or other purposes.

Advance Sheets. 1. A copy of a book, in sheets, for preliminary notices, or for simultaneous publication in two or more places, though occasionally for earlier publication in another place. Advance sheets for review purposes are generally sent as folded, but unbound, signatures. Also known as Early Sheets. 2. Sheets of a publication, as of certain serial or other documents, printed separately for use before they are issued in collected form. Strictly, these are preprints.

Advertisement File. A file of samples of advertisements, found most often in a business library.

Adviser, Readers'. *See* Readers' Adviser.

Agency, Library. *See* Library Agency.

Agent. An individual or a firm from whom books, periodicals, and other library materials are secured. Also called Purchasing Agent.

Aisle (in stack). A passageway intersecting the ranges in a stack.

Albertype (Alberttype). *See* Collotype (1).

Alcove. A recessed portion of a room formed by wall construction or by the projection of bookcases at right angles to the wall or some partition, generally with room for a table and chairs.

Alcove System. A method of storing books in wall and floor cases around alcoves, the arrangement often extending for two or three stories.

All Along. In hand sewing of books,

with the thread passing from kettle stitch to kettle stitch of successive signatures, one complete course of thread going to each section. Also called One sheet on, and One on. A local alternative term is Straight on. *Cf.* Two along.

All Rights Reserved. A statement indicating that the privilege of reproducing in any form a book or any part of it will not be granted without the consent of the owner of the copyright.

Allover. A small pattern constantly repeated. In book cloths, an allover pattern runs down as well as across the roll.

Almanac. 1. An annual publication containing a calendar, frequently accompanied by astronomical data and other information. 2. An annual yearbook of statistics and other information sometimes in a particular field.

Alphabetic Classed Catalog. *See* Alphabetico-classed Catalog.

Alphabetic-classed Filing System. A grouping of material into broad subject classes alphabetically arranged and subdivided by topics arranged alphabetically within each class.

Alphabetic Order Table. *See* Cutter Table; Cutter-Sanborn Table.

Alphabetic Subject Catalog. A catalog limited to subject entries, with the necessary references, alphabetically arranged.

Alphabetic Subject Filing System. Arrangement of material under specific subjects in alphabetical order.

Alphabetic Subject Index. An index under specific subjects arranged alphabetically, as an independent periodical index, an index to an author or a classed list of books or articles, an index to a classification scheme, or an index to a classed catalog.

Alphabetico-classed Catalog. A catalog with entries under broad subjects alphabetically arranged and subdivided by topics in alphabetical order.

Alphabetizing or Alphabeting. Arranging in alphabetical order.

Alternative Title. A subtitle introduced by "or" or its equivalent; *e.g., Hypatia; or, New foes with an old face.* [C.]

American Braille. An obsolete embossed type for the blind, a variation of braille, in which, as in the New York point, the most frequently used symbols were the simplest.

American Russia. An imitation russia made from cowhide, generally grained with a straight grain. Also called Russia Cowhide.

Americana. All material that has been printed about the Americas, printed in the Americas, or written by Americans, with frequent restriction of period to that of the formative stage in the history of the two continents or their constituent parts, the final date for North America varying from 1800 to 1820. [Reprinted from Stillwell, *Incunabula and Americana,* by permission of Columbia University Press.]

-ana. A suffix denoting anecdotes

and other material about a subject, generally a person or a place.

Analytic or Analytical. *See* Analytical Entry.

Analytical Entry. The entry of some part of a work or of some article contained in a collection (volume of essays, serial, etc.) including a reference to the publication which contains the article or work entered. [C.]

In special libraries it may be an entry for a significant paragraph, section, table, etc., or for a single statement or figure.

Analytical Index. 1. An alphabetical index under specific topics to information in articles arranged under general subjects, as in a reference book. 2. A classified index to material under specific subjects, as in a reference book.

Analytical Note. The statement in an analytical entry referring to the publication that contains the article or work entered.

Anastatic Printing. A method of facsimile printing by means of zinc plates given a relief printing surface through the action of acid.

Angle Bracket. *See* Bracket (*n*.).

Angle-top or Angle-tab Guide. A guide with a celluloid projection for holding a label, attached to the top edge at an angle of forty-five degrees. Also known as Tilted-tab Guide.

Annals. 1. A periodical publication recording events of a year, transactions of an organization, or progress in special fields. 2. Earlier, a record

of events arranged in chronological order. 3. In a general sense, any historical narrative.

Anniversary Issue. *See* Special Number.

Annotation. 1. A note that describes, explains, or evaluates; especially, such a note added to an entry in a bibliography, reading list, or catalog. Sometimes called Book Note. 2. The process of making such notes.

Annual. 1. A publication issued regularly once a year, as an annual report or proceedings of an organization; or, a yearly publication that reviews events or developments during a year, sometimes limited to a special field. 2. A giftbook (*q.v.*).

Anonym. 1. A person whose name is not made public. 2. A pseudonym.

Anonymous. 1. Published without the author's name in the book. 2. With author's name unknown or undisclosed.

Anonymous Classic. A work of unknown or doubtful authorship, commonly designated by title, which may have appeared in the course of time in many editions, versions, and/or translations. [C.]

Anthology. A collection of extracts from the works of various authors, sometimes limited to poetry or to a particular subject.

Antiqua. A German name for roman type.

Antique Paper. A light, bulky, uncalendered paper having a rough finish in imitation of old hand-made paper.

Antique Tooling. A form of blind tooling.

Aperture. *See* Lens Aperture. [M.]

Apocryphal Book. 1. A book of doubtful authorship or authenticity. 2. Specifically, one of the books of the Old Testament Apocrypha or the New Testament Apocrypha.

Apograph. A copy of an original manuscript.

Appendix. Matter supplementing the text of a book but not essential to its completeness, as a bibliography, statistical tables, and explanatory material.

Application Card. A printed form which a person fills out to become a library borrower.

Application File. Signed application cards arranged in order, usually alphabetical. Sometimes called Borrowers' File, Borrowers' Register, and Registration File.

Apprentice. A person without previous library training who is admitted to a staff to learn the routines of a particular library through actual work and instruction, often working without pay.

Apprentice Class. A group receiving brief, systematic training in a library for the lower grades of library work through directed practice and instruction by members of the staff.

Apprentices' Library. *See* Mechanics' Library.

Approved Library School. A school for library education, or some other training agency, recognized by a state certification board or an educational agency as meeting its standards, irrespective of accreditation by the American Library Association.

Aquatint. 1. A method of etching that produces tones as a network of white dots, through the application of powdered resin to the plate before it is eaten by acid. 2. A print so produced.

Aquatone. *See* Collotype (1).

Arabesque. A style of binding ornamentation marked by interlacing straight and curved lines; derived from Arabian decorative designs.

Archives. 1. (A collective noun used properly only in the plural.) The organized body of records made or received in connection with the transaction of its affairs by a government or a governmental agency, an institution, organization, or establishment, or a family or individual, and preserved for record purposes in its custody or that of its legal successors. 2. An institution for the preservation and servicing of noncurrent archival material.

Archivist. A person engaged in the preservation or servicing of noncurrent archival material.

Armorial Bookplate. A bookplate bearing a coat of arms.

Art File. *See* Picture or Art File.

Art Vellum. A brand name for a lightweight book cloth.

Artcraft. A term used by some publishers to designate an artificial-leather edition binding. Used to avoid the designations "artificial-leather" and "imitation-leather."

Artist's Proof. A proof of an engraving, usually with the signature of the artist in pencil, and sometimes with a small sketch, known as a remarque, in the margin. Also called Remarque Proof.

Artotype. *See* Collotype (1).

Ascender. 1. That part of a lower-case letter that projects above the body. 2. A lower-case letter with a part that extends above its body, as b, f, h.

Assigned Reading Room. *See* Reserved Book Department (1).

Assignment Notification Blank. A printed or mimeographed slip to be filled out with teacher's name, date, and subject, as an advance notice to a school librarian of detailed assignments requiring use of library material.

Assistant. A subordinate staff member. The word is frequently combined with the name of a department or a personnel term denoting type of service, as circulation assistant, assistant cataloger; or with a term indicating rank, as first assistant, senior assistant.

Assistant Librarian. 1. An associate librarian (*q.v.*). 2. A librarian, or one of several librarians, ranking next to the chief librarian or the associate librarian, and generally in charge of a particular part of the library's work, or the activities of a group of departments.

Associate. A staff member delegated to assist in the discharge of a particular function, often with administrative authority, but not in charge of the service.

Associate Librarian. The one member of a library staff who ranks next to the librarian and whose work is chiefly administrative.

Association Copy. A book that gives evidence, through bookplate, special binding, autograph, presentation inscription, or marginal or other notes, of having had some special connection with the author, some distinguished individual, or a celebrated library or collection.

Copies signed by the author for the trade, as a help to the sale of the book, are not considered true association copies.

Association Library. A library owned or controlled by the members of an association which elects the governing board. The governing board may or may not include municipal representatives. Membership is usually obtained by subscriptions to annual or life memberships, and service may be limited to members or persons designated by them, or may be provided free to the community.

Association Publication. *See* Society Publication.

Asyndetic. Without cross references; said of a catalog.

Athenaeum. A name given to certain proprietary libraries, reading rooms, or buildings used as libraries, particularly in New England in the early part of the nineteenth century.

Atlas. A volume of maps, plates, engravings, tables, etc., with or without descriptive letterpress. It may be an independent publication or it may have been issued to accompany one or more volumes of text. [C.]

Attendant. A person on duty in a library room or at a library desk.

Auction Catalog. A catalog of books from one or more private libraries offered for sale at auction.

Audio-visual Materials. Aids to teaching through ear and eye, such as phonograph records, slides, and motion-picture films.

Author. 1. The writer of a book, as distinguished from the translator, editor, etc. 2. In the broader sense, the maker of the book or the person or body immediately responsible for its existence. Thus, a person who collects and puts together the writings of several authors (compiler or editor) may be said to be the author of a collection. A corporate body may be considered the author of publications issued in its name or by its authority. [C.]

Author Abbreviation. *See* Secondary Fulness.

Author Affiliation. In some special libraries, a statement on catalog cards of the organization with which each author is connected, thus indicating his experience and point of view.

Author Analytic. An entry under author for a part of a work or of some article contained in a collection (volume of essays, serial, etc.) including a reference to the publication which contains the article or work entered.

Author and Title Catalog. A catalog consisting of author and title entries, and sometimes entries for editors, translators, series, etc., but excluding subject entries.

Author Authority Card. *See* Authority Card.

Author Bibliography. A list of the books and articles by, or by and about, an author.

Author Card. A catalog card containing an author entry.

Author Catalog. An alphabetical catalog of author entries and author added entries such as editors, translators, etc.

Author Entry. An entry of a work in a catalog under its author's name as heading, whether this be a main or an added heading. The author heading may consist of a personal or a corporate name or some substitute for it, *e.g.,* initials, pseudonym, etc. [C.]

Author Fulness. The full form of an author's name used in author entries in a catalog, as distinguished from secondary fulness.

Author Heading. The form under which an author entry is made.

Author Indention. *See* "First" Indention.

Author Number. A combination of letters and figures assigned to each book for the purpose of preserving on the shelves an alphabetical arrangement by author under each class.

Author Style. The use in author headings of black capitals and lower-case letters. *Cf.* Subject Style.

Author Table. *See* Cutter Table; Cutter-Sanborn Table.

Authority Card. An official card that gives the form selected for a heading in a catalog. If the heading is for a personal author, it has references to sources and a record of variant forms; if for a corporate author, sources, a brief history, and a statement about changes of name. Sometimes called Information Card. *Cf.* History Card.

Authority List or File. An official list of forms selected as headings in a catalog, giving for author and corporate names and for the forms of entry of anonymous classics the sources used for establishing the forms, together with the variant forms. If the list is a name list, it is sometimes called Name List and Name File.

Authorized Edition. An edition issued with the consent of the author or the representative to whom he may have delegated his rights and privileges.

Author's Edition. 1. An edition of the collected or complete works of an author uniformly bound and having a collective title. 2. An edition authorized by the author.

Author's Proof. A proof after correction of compositor's errors, sent to the author for his correction.

Autobiography. A history of a person's life written by himself.

Autograph. 1. A manuscript in the author's own handwriting. 2. A signature.

Automatic Book Carrier. *See* Book Conveyor.

Automatic Book Charging. *See* Charging Machine.

Automatic Book Delivery. A method of conveying library books from the stacks to the delivery desk by an endless-belt device.

Automatic Routing. In a special library, a plan whereby each issue of a periodical is automatically sent as it is received to a prearranged list of persons in the organization served by the library.

Autonym. A person's real name; or a work published under it.

Azure Tooling. A binding decoration consisting of parallel lines or bars; derived from the use of thin horizontal lines in heraldry to indicate blue.

Back. 1. The combined back edges of a volume, as secured together and shaped for covering. *Cf.* Backbone, Spine, Shelf Back, Backstrip. 2. Short for backbone, shelf back, and backstrip.

Back Edge. The left-hand edge of a recto, corresponding to the right-hand edge of a verso. This is the binding edge in the case of the ordinary bound book.

Back File. Numbers of a periodical preceding the current issue.

Back Lining. 1. Generally, the material used to line the back of a book prior to encasing it in a loose back (or hollow back) cover. 2. The muslin reinforcement on the back of some paper-covered books. 3. Sometimes, in library binding, the paper used for stiffening the backbone of the cover. The preferred term for this is "inlay."

Back Margin. The left-hand margin of a printed recto and the right-hand margin of a printed verso. In the ordinary book, the back margin is contiguous to the binding edge. Also known as Inner Margin, Inside Margin, Gutter Margin.

Back Number. Any issue of a periodical or newspaper preceding the current issue.

Backbone. That portion of the cover of a bound volume which stands exposed when ranged with others on a shelf in the usual way. Also called Spine, Shelf Back, and Back.

Backstrip. 1. The spine (q.v.) of a book. Sometimes called Back. 2. That portion of a cover material which extends from joint to joint. Sometimes called Back. 3. Erroneous usage for Inlay (def. 1) (q.v.).

Ballopticon. A projection apparatus by which the image is projected by light reflected from the object. [M.]

Banding. A binding decoration consisting of bands.

Bands. 1. The cords or tapes on which the sections of a book are sewed, when not let into prepared saw cuts across the back. 2. The ridges across the backbone of certain leather-bound volumes. 3. Loosely, gold-creased lines across the backbone.

Bank Letter. A bulletin issued at regular intervals by a bank, usually on general financial and business conditions.

Banned Book. A publication censored by a government, an institution, or a religious organization because of its content or the beliefs and activities of its author, usually on patriotic, moral, or religious grounds.

Base. 1. A substance that has an alkaline chemical reaction; it reacts with acids to form salts. 2. A substance that has been coated with a light-sensitive material to form a photographic film, i.e., cellulose nitrate, cellulose acetate, or glass. [M.]

Basket. See Bucket.

Bastard Title. See Half Title (1).

Battledore. An early form of primer, made of folded paper or cardboard, generally varnished on the inside, which, opened out, resembled in shape a hornbook without a handle. Sometimes called Hornbook.

Bead. An old term for headband.

Beading. The twist of the silk in

headbands; so called from its resemblance to a series of beads.

Ben Day Process. A mechanical process for producing shaded tints on a printing plate by the use of gelatine films or screens marked with a variety of patterns.

Bench Sewing. Sewing through the fold by hand on the sewing bench, to suspended cords, or tapes, arranged crosswise along the back edges.

Best Books. A group of books considered as most desirable or most authoritative in the several fields of knowledge or in a particular field.

Best Seller. A current popular book in most active demand in book stores. In a broader sense, a standard book having a steady sale over a period of years.

Bevelled Boards. Bevel-edged binding boards, now seldom used except for very large books. The top, front, and bottom edges only are bevelled.

Bible Paper. A very thin, strong paper used for printing Bibles and other books requiring many pages in compact form.

Bible Style. A term commonly used to designate any flexible round-cornered leather binding.

Biblia Pauperum. Literally, Bible of the Poor. A type of medieval picture book, in either manuscript or printed form, containing illustrations of Scriptural subjects, with descriptive texts. It was one of the earliest block books.

Bibliographer. 1. A person familiar with methods of describing the physical characteristics of books, who prepares bibliographies, catalogs, and lists. 2. One who writes about books, especially in regard to their authorship, date, typography, editions, etc.; one skilled in bibliography. [Def. 2, by permission; from *The Century Dictionary and Cyclopedia*, copyright, 1895, by the Century Co.]

Bibliographical Ghost. A book or an edition of a book, recorded in bibliographies or otherwise mentioned, of whose existence there is no reasonable proof. Also called Ghost.

Bibliographical Note. 1. A note, often a footnote, containing a reference to one or more works used as sources for the work. 2. A note in a catalog or a bibliography, relating to the bibliographical history or description of a book. 3. A note in a catalog mentioning a bibliography (often in the form of footnotes) contained in the book.

Bibliography. 1. The study of the material form of books, with comparison of variations in issues and copies, as a means of determining the history and transmission of texts. 2. The art of describing books correctly with respect to authorship, editions, physical form, etc. 3. The preparation of lists of books, maps, etc. 4. A list of books, maps, etc., differing from a catalog in not being necessarily a list of materials in a collection, a library, or a group of libraries.

Bibliology. The science of books, embracing knowledge of the physical book in all its aspects, as printing, bookbinding, bookselling, libraries, and library science. Bibliography in its widest sense.

Bibliomania. An intense desire for acquiring books.

Bibliophile. A lover of books, especially of their format. [By permission; from Webster's *New International Dictionary,* Second Edition, copyright, 1934, 1939, by G. & C. Merriam Co.]

Bill. A draft of a proposed law introduced in a legislative body.

Bill Drafting. In legislative reference libraries, the writing of a legislative bill, in which the library cooperates with the drafting department by gathering and preparing information needed.

Bimonthly. (*n.*) A publication issued every two months.

Bin. An open or a closed compartment of a shelf, designed to hold a current issue or several recent issues of a periodical. Also called Pigeonhole.

Bind In. To fasten securely into the binding; said of supplementary material.

Binder. A container of heavy paper, pasteboard, or boards for protecting pamphlets, magazines, or clippings. Also called Cover.

Binder's Board. A high-quality single-ply, solid pulp board for bookbinding, made to full thickness in one operation, from mixed papers, and kiln-dried or plate-dried. Sometimes called Millboard.

Binder's Date. The date on the back of a bound serial publication placed there by the binder.

Binder's Slip. *See* Binding Slip.

Binder's Title. The title lettered on the book by the binder, as distinguished from the title on the publisher's original binding or cover. *Cf.* Cover Title. [C.]

Bindery. An establishment that specializes in one or another of the various kinds of bookbinding.

Bindery Department. *See* Binding or Bindery Department.

Bindery Record. *See* Binding or Bindery Record.

Bindery Slip. *See* Binding Slip.

Binding. 1. The process of producing a single volume from leaves, sheets, signatures, or issues of periodicals, or of covering such a volume. 2. The finished work produced by this process. 3. The cover of a volume.

Binding Book. A register in which the books sent to a binder for binding are recorded, with particulars as to lettering, style, color, etc.

Binding or Bindery Department. 1. The department that prepares books, periodicals, and other material for binding or rebinding. 2. A bindery maintained by a library.

Binding Edge. The edge of a volume, usually the back edge, that is to receive the main binding treatment (sewing, rounding-and-backing, etc.).

Binding Proof. A few rough edges left on a trimmed volume to show that it has not been cut down excessively. Also called Proof.

Binding or Bindery Record. A temporary or a permanent list of periodicals, other serials, and sets of books, sent to a bindery, with data as to title, style of binding, etc.

Binding Slip. A slip of paper containing instructions for handling the particular item which accompanies it to the bindery. Also called Binder's Slip, Bindery Slip, and Specification Slip.

Biobibliography. A list of books by many authors which includes brief biographical data about them.

Biographee. The person who is the subject of a biography.

Biography. 1. A history of the life of an individual. 2. Collectively, histories of the lives of individuals; or, the branch of literature devoted to such writings.

Biography or Who's Who File. A card file, or a collection of clippings, etc., giving information about individuals.

Biscoe Time Number. A book number expressing a date in abbreviated form, from a scheme devised by W. S. Biscoe for arranging books on shelves chronologically rather than alphabetically. Sometimes called Biscoe Date Letter.

Black Letter. *See* Gothic (2).

Blackface (or Black-faced Type). *See* Boldface (or Bold-faced Type).

Blanket. *See* Blanket Sheet.

Blanket Sheet. A folio-sized newspaper, with four pages from one folding of the sheet. Also called Blanket.

Blanking. The stamping of a design on a cover without the use of ink or gilt, done by means of a heated brass die. Also called Blind Stamping.

Bleed. 1. To trim printed matter so that the text or illustration is cut into. 2. Of printing, especially illustrations, to run to the extreme edge of the page, leaving no margin.

Bleed Illustration. An illustration printed so that it runs to the extreme edge of the page, leaving no margin.

Blind Reference. A reference in a catalog, bibliography, or index from one heading to another under which no entry is found.

Blind Stamping. The stamping of an impression on a book cover without the use of gilt or some coloring material. Also called Embossing. *Cf.* Blind Tooling.

Blind Tooling. 1. The process of tooling a design on the cover of a book without putting on gilt, sometimes preliminary to gold tooling on the design. 2. The design thus produced on the cover.

Block. 1. A piece of wood engraved for printing or stamping. 2. A piece of wood or metal on which is fastened a stereotype or other printing plate.

Block Accession. To accession books by lots, assigning a group of consecutive numbers to the books without giving particular numbers to individual books.

Block Arrangement or Plan. A method of shelving books in a library in a regular shelf-to-shelf, case-to-case order according to classification.

Block Book. A book printed from wooden blocks cut in relief, with illustrations and text for each page on one block, a type of book common at about the time of the introduction of printing. Also known as Xylographic Book, and, in the plural, as Xylographica.

Block Letter. *See* Sans-serif.

Block Plan. *See* Block Arrangement or Plan.

Block Print. A print made from a wood, linoleum, or metal block cut in relief.

Block System. The sending of library units to school classrooms to suit curriculum needs, with frequent changes of titles. Also called Fluid Unit System.

Blue Book. 1. A popular name for a government publication issued in a blue cover. 2. A popular name for a government publication that lists officials and gives other data about the government organization, *e.g.*, a state manual. 3. In Great Britain, a title applied to official reports of Parliament and the Privy Council, which are issued in blue paper covers.

Blue Paper. A popular name for a daily record issued to members of the British Parliament reporting transactions of the preceding day in the House of Commons, with notices of new business. Issued in a blue cover.

Blurb. A description and recommendation of a book prepared by the publisher and appearing generally on the book jacket.

Board. The binder's board, pasted board, chip board, news board, and laminated board used as a foundation for book covers. So called because wood was originally used.

Board of Trustees. The governing board of a library. Also known as Library Board, Board of Directors, and Library Trustees.

Board Paper. *See* Paste-down.

Boards. A form of bookbinding in which the boards are covered with paper. Also called Paper Boards. *Cf.* In boards.

Bock. A kind of sheepskin leather, sometimes used as a substitute for morocco.

Body of a Book. The main part of a book that follows introductory matter and precedes appendixes and notes.

Body Type. Type used for reading matter, as in the body of a book, as distinguished from display type, used in headings, display lines in advertisements, etc.

Boldface (or Bold-faced Type). Type with lines made broader than normal. Also called Blackface (or Black-faced

Type). Formerly called Fatface (or Fat-faced Type).

Bolt. A fold of the paper at the top edge, fore edge, or occasionally the foot, of an uncut or an unopened book.

Bone Folder. A flat piece of bone six or eight inches long and about one inch wide, used for folding paper and in book repairing.

Book. 1. A collection of tablets of wood or ivory, of sheets of paper, parchment, or similar material, blank, written, or printed, strung or bound together; commonly, many folded and bound sheets, containing continuous printing or writing; esp., when printed, a bound volume, or a volume of some size, as distinguished from a pamphlet. 2. A volume without a cover; an uncased volume, whether partly bound or not; the assembled pages considered apart from their enclosing case. 3. A literary composition; esp., a long systematic one. 4. A major division of a treatise or literary work. [By permission; from Webster's *New International Dictionary*, Second Edition, copyright, 1934, 1939, by G. & C. Merriam Co.]

Book Automobile. *See* Bookmobile.

Book Box. *See* Cumdach.

Book Brace. *See* Book Support.

Book Capacity. *See* Shelf Capacity.

Book Car. *See* Bookmobile.

Book Card. A card placed in a book to be used in charging it. Sometimes called Book Slip, Charge Slip, and Charging Slip.

Book Card File. *See* Charging File. (1).

Book Carriage. A single platform, or two reciprocating spring platforms, on which a book is held by clamps for microfilming. The platform slides back and forth on a runway to bring opposite pages of the book into the field of exposure. [M.]

Book Carrier. *See* Book Conveyor.

Book Carrier, Pneumatic. *See* Pneumatic Book Carrier.

Book Charging Machine. *See* Charging Machine.

Book Chute. *See* Chute.

Book Cloth. Cotton or linen cloth (colored, sized, glazed, and/or embossed or otherwise processed) designed for book covers.

Book Conveyor. A mechanical device for carrying books from place to place, which operates horizontally or vertically on the endless-chain principle. Also called Automatic Book Carrier, Book Carrier, Book Distributor.

Book Cover. *See* Cover.

Book Cradle. *See* Bookholder. [M.]

Book Display Case. *See* Display Case.

Book Display Rack. *See* Display Case (1); Rack.

Book Distributor. *See* Book Conveyor.

Book Drive. A systematic intensive campaign to stimulate gifts of books to increase the collections of a library or for some other purpose.

Book Elevator. *See* Book Lift.

Book End. *See* Book Support.

Book Fair. An exhibit of books sponsored by a group of booksellers and publishers, a library, or some other group, or by a combination of such agencies; in Europe conducted by booksellers and publishers as a book market.

Book Hand. The handwriting used by scribes in preparing manuscript books before the introduction of printing, as distinguished from the cursive hand used for letters, documents, and other records.

Book Hunter. A book collector, especially one who searches for old and rare publications.

Book Jacket. A detachable wrapper, plain or printed, flush with the covers at head and tail, but folded over between the cover (both front and back) and the book proper. Also called Dust Cover, Dust Jacket, Dust Wrapper, Jacket, Jacket Cover, and Wrapper.

Book Lift. A machine for carrying books from one floor or stack level to another, operated by hand or by power on the dumb-waiter principle. Also known as Book Elevator.

Book List. A select list of titles in a library, or a publisher's list of books, often with descriptive notes to aid in selection.

Book Mark. *See* Book Number.

Book Note. *See* Annotation (1).

Book Number. A combination of letters and figures used to arrange books in the same classification number in alphabetical order. It usually consists of an author number and a work mark. Occasionally called Book Mark.

Book of Hours. A medieval liturgical book, containing prayers, Psalms, and other devotional exercises, for reciting at the canonical hours; often a beautifully illuminated book.

Book Paper. Paper used principally in the manufacture of books and magazines, as distinguished from newsprint, and writing and cover papers.

Book Piracy. *See* Pirated Edition.

Book Pocket. A pocket of stiff paper, an envelope, or a slip of paper, pasted on the inside of a book cover to hold a book card or a borrower's card. Also called Card Pocket and Pocket.

Book Press. *See* Bookcase; Press.

Book Press (Binding and Repair). A device for pressing books.

Book Record. A record of books charged that shows by whom a book has been borrowed and when it is due.

Book Rack. *See* Rack.

Book Repair Department. *See* Repair Department.

Book Return Cabinet. *See* Bookbin (1).

Book Review. *See* Review (1).

Book Room. A room containing the principal book collection of a library. *Cf.* Stack.

Book Selection. 1. The process of choosing books for library collections. 2. A library school course on the principles underlying the choice of material for various kinds of libraries and types of readers.

Book Shrine. *See* Cumdach.

Book Size. *See* Size (Books).

Book Slip. *See* Book Card.

Book Stack. *See* Stack.

Book Stock. A library's book collection.

Book Support. A device of metal or wood to support a row of books. Also called Brace, Book Brace, and Book End.

Book Trade Journal. A periodical issued by publishers or booksellers, individually or collectively, calling attention to books published or for sale, and sometimes including information about book production and distribution and a current record of new books.

Book Tray. A low box for carrying books. It has three sides and is provided with handles or perforations in the sides to facilitate handling.

Book Trough. A V-shaped wooden shelf or rack for the display of books, often a part of a counter or loan desk.

Book Truck. A small vehicle on wheels provided with two or three shelves, used for transporting books within a building.

Book Turnover. The number of books circulated by a library or some unit of service during a fiscal period divided by the number of volumes in its collection.

Book Wagon. *See* Bookmobile.

Book Week. 1. A week in November set aside for special celebration and exhibits by booksellers, librarians, and other groups, to stimulate interest in books and reading for children and young people. 2. A week set aside for special celebration and exhibits by booksellers, librarians, and other groups, to stimulate interest in books in a particular field, as Catholic Book Week, Jewish Book Week, Religious Book Week.

Bookbin. 1. A box or cabinet on wheels for moving books. Also called a Book Return Cabinet. 2. A space in a loan desk in which books are placed while waiting for later discharging routine.

Bookbinding. *See* Binding.

Bookcase. A case with shelves for books.

Bookholder. Usually, a box with hinged glass top and two reciprocating spring platforms within, used to hold bound materials immovable and flat while being microfilmed. [M.]

Booklet. A small book, usually with paper covers; or a pamphlet.

Bookmark. A piece of paper or other material to be slipped between the leaves of a book to mark a place. Also called Bookmarker and Marker. *Cf.* Register.

Bookmarker. *See* Bookmark.

Bookmobile. An automobile truck especially equipped to carry books and serve as a traveling branch library. Also called Book Automobile, Book Car, and Book Wagon.

Bookplate. A label pasted in a book to indicate ownership and, sometimes, location in a library.

Bookrest. A device for holding a book at a convenient angle for reading.

Books for the Blind. Books prepared for reading by the blind. They are either embossed or recorded; *e.g.,* books in braille or moon type, and talking books.

Bookworm. 1. The larvae of various insects that injure old and unused books by working in leather bindings and boring small holes in the leaves. 2. A person devoted to books who reads voraciously.

Border. 1. An ornamental design along one or more sides of a page of an illuminated manuscript or of any body of printed matter, or surrounding an illuminated miniature. 2. A binding ornamentation that runs close

to the edges of the sides and, respectively, the spine, of a volume. To be distinguished from Frame.

Borrower. A person to whom a library lends books. Also called Card Holder.

Borrower's Card. A card issued to a borrower on which a record of books borrowed by him is kept. Also called Library Card and Reader's Card.

Borrower's Card Number. *See* Borrower's Number.

Borrowers' File. *See* Application File; Registration Record or File.

Borrower's Number. The registration number assigned to a library patron. Also known as Borrower's Card Number.

Borrower's Pocket. An envelope marked with a borrower's name, used in charging books by the Browne charging system.

Borrower's Record. Entries under a borrower's name or number showing all books charged to him, usually with dates of issue and return.

Borrowers' Register. *See* Application File; Registration Record or File.

Boss. A metal binding ornament on a cover to protect it from wear, usually placed at the corners and the center.

Boston Line. *See* Line Letter Type.

Bound Volume. Any book that is bound; usually, a volume of a periodical in bound form.

"Bound With." *See* Independent.

Bowdlerize. To expurgate the text of a book by omitting or changing objectionable words or passages; from the name of Thomas Bowdler, who in 1818 issued an expurgated edition of Shakespeare.

Box Edge. *See* Divinity Circuit.

Box Pocket. A stiffened three-dimensional pocket.

Boxed. Enclosed in a box-like protective container for display purposes or to keep several units together; said of a set of books.

Brace. *See* Book Support.

Bracket. (*n.*) One of the small rectangular marks [ ] used in cataloging to enclose information supplied; called a square bracket. One of the angular marks < > used in cataloging to enclose matter that appears in square brackets on a title page; called an angle bracket. (*v.*) To enclose in brackets.

Bracket Shelf. A stack shelf attached to uprights by brackets that carry the shelf in cantilever fashion.

Braille. A system of embossed print for the blind, that uses all the combinations of six dots arranged in groups or cells, three dots high and two dots wide; perfected and put into its present form by Louis Braille, a blind Frenchman. Braille is now in four grades: grade one, grade one and a half, grade two, and grade three.

Braille, Grade One. Braille that contains no contractions, but has all words spelled in full.

Braille, Grade One and a Half. A braille containing forty-four contractions, used only in the United States; so called because it is intermediate between grades one and two of the English braille.

Braille, Grade Two. In England prior to 1932, braille having nearly two hundred contractions; since then superseded in England and America by Standard English Braille, grade two.

Braille, Grade Three. An amplification of braille, grade two, in which many additional contractions are used. Practically no reading matter in this grade is available in this country to date. It is used only by a small number of students and professional persons.

Braille: Standard English Braille, Grades One and Two. The braille system as adopted and authorized in 1932 by the British National Uniform Type Committee and the American Committee on Grade Two. It is a modification of the braille system as used in England prior to 1932, with a few contractions omitted, a few added, and the rules governing the use of contractions somewhat changed.

Braille Music Notation. A system of embossed music symbols based on the braille character used in braille print.

Braille Slate or Tablet. A device for writing braille consisting of two metal blades, one pitted with rows of braille cells, the other with openings to locate the pitted cells. Paper is inserted between the blades and the dots are made with a stylus, moving from right to left.

Braille Writing Machine or Typewriter. A machine for writing braille, having six keys corresponding to the six dots of the braille cell.

Branch. *See* Branch Library.

Branch Department. The administrative unit of a library that supervises the work of branches and subbranches.

Branch Librarian. The administrative head of a branch library.

Branch Library. An auxiliary library with separate quarters, a permanent basic collection of books, a permanent staff, and a regular schedule. Also called Branch.

Branch Registration. *See* Central Registration; Separate Registration.

Branch Shelf List. 1. A shelf list in a branch library. 2. A union shelf list in a central library of books in the branches, subbranches, and other agencies.

Bray Library. *See* Parish Library (2).

Break. A parting of adjacent sections of a book caused by loosening of the sewing.

Broad Classification. 1. Arrangement of subjects in a classification system in broad general divisions with a mini-

mum of subdivision. 2. A method of classifying that places material in inclusive divisions rather than in minute subdivisions of a classification scheme.

Broadsheet. *See* Broadside.

Broadside. A publication consisting of a single sheet (or less frequently, of a few conjoining sheets) bearing matter printed as a single page, on one side only of the sheet; usually intended to be posted, publicly distributed, or sold, *e.g.*, proclamations, handbills, ballad sheets, newssheets, sheet calendars, etc. Usually, though not necessarily, of quarto size or larger. Not synonymous with broadsheet, which by several authorities is used to designate a single sheet publication with each side printed as a single page. [C.]

Brochure. A short printed work, consisting of only a few leaves, merely stitched together with thread or cord and not otherwise bound. Literally, a stitched work (from the French *brocher,* to stitch).

Broken. 1. Of a book, tending to open readily at a place or places where the binding has been forced or strained. 2. Of a leaf, folded over.

Broken File. *See* Incomplete File.

Broken Over. Of plates, folded or turned over a short distance from the back edge before being placed in the volume preparatory to binding, so that the plates may lie flat and be easily turned.

Broker's Circular. A circular published by a brokerage house, sometimes at regular intervals, containing descriptions of securities, usually of new issues.

Browne Charging System. A single-entry method of recording book loans originated by Nina E. Browne, which uses a pocket bearing the borrower's name to hold the book card of each book borrowed. The system is little used today.

Brown's Adjustable Classification. *See* Adjustable Classification.

Brown's Subject Classification. *See* Subject Classification.

Browsing Period. *See* Free Reading Period.

Browsing Room. A comfortably and attractively furnished room in a library, with a collection of books for cultural and recreational reading.

Brussels Classification. *See* Classification Décimale Universelle.

Bucket. That part of a book conveyor in which books or conveyor trays are placed for transport. Sometimes called Basket.

Buckram. A filled book cloth with a heavy-weave cotton base. Originally applied only to a starch-filled fabric of this type; now also, loosely, any filled fabric with a heavy base.

Buffing. A thin split of leather, usually cowhide but sometimes sheepskin; any split, other than the flesh side, usually the top or grain.

Building Department. The person or

persons responsible for the maintenance of the buildings and equipment of a large library system, and sometimes the supervision of janitorial work. Also called Maintenance Department and Operations Department.

Bulletin. A publication issued at regular intervals by a government department, a society, or an institution, usually numbered.

Burnished Edges. Colored or gilded edges that have been polished, usually with a bloodstone or an agate.

Business Branch. A branch of a public library easily accessible to the downtown section, furnishing for business and commercial interests of a city a working collection of books, directories, services, and other pertinent materials.

Business Firm Borrower's Card. A card issued to a corporation, on which are charged books for the use of the organization. Sometimes called Corporation Card and Firm Card.

By Authority. Published by permission of a legally constituted official or body.

Cabinet, Card. *See* Card Cabinet.

Cadastral Map. A large-scale map or survey showing ownership and value of land, for use in apportioning taxes.

Calendar. 1. A chronological list of documents, with annotations indicating or summarizing the contents of each. 2. A schedule of events or discussions in the order in which they are to take place, as of cases in court or of bills in a legislative body.

Calendered Paper. A paper with a smooth and glossy or a watered appearance produced by the paper's passing between the rotating heated rolls of a specially constructed machine called a calender.

Calf. A smooth leather made from calfskin.

Calf Finish. The smooth, ungrained finish of any animal skin tanned for bookbinding purposes.

Calf Split. A split leather made from a calfskin. It is sometimes made with an embossed surface so as to resemble the original hair side of the skin.

Call Card. A card that combines the functions of a book card and a call slip in a single-file charging system.

Call Mark. *See* Call Number.

Call Number. Letters, figures, and symbols, separate or in combination, assigned to a book to indicate its location on shelves. It usually consists of class number and book number. Sometimes known as Call Mark.

Call Slip. A form which a borrower fills out when he wishes to borrow a book or to use a book not on open shelves.

Call Station. *See* Delivery Station; Deposit Station.

Calligraphy. The art of beautiful writing. [By permission; from *The*

Century Dictionary and Cyclopedia, copyright, 1895, by the Century Co.]

Cameo Binding. A style of binding having the center of the boards stamped in relief, in imitation of antique gems or medals.

Camaïeu. *See* Chiaroscuro.

Cancel. Any part of a book (a leaf or leaves, or part of a leaf) intended to be substituted for the corresponding part of the book as originally printed. Called also Cancelans, and one such leaf a Canceling Leaf. A cancel for only part of a leaf now usually takes the form of a correction slip to be pasted on the original leaf, which is not removed. The term cancel applies only to the new part, and not to the part which it is intended to replace. [C.]

Cancelandum. *See* Canceled leaf.

Cancelans. *See* Cancel.

Canceled Leaf, Leaves, Signatures, etc. The part of a book intended to be replaced by a cancel. Called also Cancelandum. [C.]

Canceling Leaf. *See* Cancel.

Capacity. *See* Conveyor Capacity; Shelf Capacity; Stack Capacity.

Cape Morocco. A morocco made from Cape (South African) goatskins.

Capital Writing. Ancient writing in Latin manuscripts, which consisted wholly of capital letters.

Capsa. A cylindrical box used in Roman libraries to hold one or more rolls standing upright.

Caption. The heading at the beginning of the text or of a chapter, section, article, etc. *Cf.* Running Title, Headline. [C.]

Caption Title. The title of a work given at the beginning of the first page of the text. Called also Head Title, Text Title, or Drop-down Title. [C.]

Card. (*n.*) A piece of cardboard used in making a library record. (*v.*) *See* Slip.

Card, Borrower's. *See* Borrower's Card.

Card Cabinet. A case of drawers or trays for storage of cards.

Card Catalog. A catalog in which entries are on separate cards arranged in a definite order in drawers.

Card Catalog Cabinet. *See* Card Catalog Case.

Card Catalog Case. A filing cabinet of drawers or trays for holding a card catalog. Also called Card Catalog Cabinet and Catalog Case.

Card Drawer. *See* Card Tray.

Card Frame. *See* Label Holder.

Card Holder. *See* Borrower.

Card Number (Catalog cards). A number, or a combination of a letter, letters, or a date and a number, that identifies a particular card in a stock

of printed catalog cards, such as Library of Congress cards.

Card Number (Circulation). *See* Borrower's Number.

Card Pocket. *See* Book Pocket.

Card Repertory. *See* Union Catalog.

Card Tray. A drawer for holding cards in a card cabinet. Also called Card Drawer, and in a card catalog case, Catalog Drawer and Catalog Tray.

Card Tray (Circulation). *See* Charging Tray.

Carnegie Library. One of the library buildings provided through funds given by Andrew Carnegie.

Carolingian. Relating to a variety of handwriting developed under the influence of Charlemagne that employed capitals, uncials, half-uncials, and minuscules.

Carrel (Carrell). An alcove for individual study in a library stack, formed by partitions or arrangement of shelving. Also called Cubicle and Stall.

Cartographer. One who prepares maps or charts, either by compilation or from original investigation and surveys.

Cartouche. A scroll-shaped or other ornamental design, with a space containing an inscription, as on an old map.

Cartridge. 1. A case, usually of leather or metal, for carrying readers' slips, books, etc., through pneumatic tubes. 2. A container for a roll of film that allows daylight loading of a camera. [M.]

Cartulary (Chartulary). 1. A collection of charters, deeds, and other records, as of a monastery. 2. A register in which these are recorded. 3. A printed copy of such records.

Case (Binding). 1. A book cover that is made complete before it is affixed to a book. 2. A slipcase (*q.v.*).

Case (Shelving). *See* Bookcase.

Case Binding. A method of binding in which the book cover is made wholly separate from the book and later attached to it; distinguished from those methods in which the cover cannot be constructed as a separate unit. Sometimes called Casework.

Case Book. 1. A volume bound in a case binding. 2. (Usually Casebook.) A book that records for study and reference real cases in law, sociology, psychology, or other fields.

Casework. *See* Case Binding.

Catalog. A list of books, maps, etc., arranged according to some definite plan. As distinguished from a bibliography it is a list which records, describes, and indexes the resources of a collection, a library, or a group of libraries. [C.]

In a special library it may include entries for material outside the library and for various types of material, *e.g.*, entries for abstracts of periodical articles and pamphlets, and entries under subject for research in progress and for organizations and individuals who are authoritative sources of information on specific subjects.

Catalog Card. 1. One of the cards composing a card catalog. 2. A plain or a ruled card, generally of standard size, 7.5 cm. high and 12.5 cm. wide, to be used for entries in a catalog or some other record.

Catalog Card Copy. *See* Process Slip.

Catalog Case. *See* Card Catalog Case.

Catalog Code. A body of rules for the entry of books, maps, etc., in a catalog.

Catalog or Cataloging Department. 1. The administrative unit of a library in charge of preparing the catalog, and, in many libraries, of classifying the books. 2. The library quarters where the cataloging processes are carried on.

Catalog Drawer. *See* Card Tray.

Catalog Slip. *See* Process Slip.

Catalog Tray. *See* Card Tray.

Cataloger. A librarian who determines the forms of entry and prepares the bibliographical descriptions for a catalog, and, in many libraries, classifies the books and assigns subject headings.

Cataloger's Slip. *See* Process Slip.

Cataloging. The process of preparing a catalog, or entries for a catalog. In a broad sense, all the processes connected with the preparation and maintaining of a catalog, including classification and assignment of subject headings. In a narrower sense, the determining of the forms of entry and preparing the bibliographical descriptions for a catalog.

Cataloging, Centralized. *See* Centralized Cataloging.

Cataloging, Cooperative. *See* Cooperative Cataloging.

Cataloging, Descriptive. *See* Descriptive Cataloging.

Cataloging, Subject. *See* Subject Cataloging.

Cataloging Department. *See* Catalog or Cataloging Department.

Cataloging Process Slip. *See* Process Slip.

Catalogue Raisonné. *See* Classed Catalog.

Catch Letters. A group of letters at the top of a page indicating the first or last word of a page or a column in a reference book such as a dictionary.

Catch Stitch. In bookbinding, any kind of lock stitch or kettle stitch.

Catchword. 1. The word (or part of a word) given at the foot of a page or at the foot of the last verso of a gathering, below the end of the last line, anticipating the first word of the page or leaf following. Rarely found in modern books. [C.] 2. A word placed at the top of a page or a column, repeating the first or the last heading of the page or the column, as in a dictionary. Also called Guide Word, Key Word, and Direction Word. 3. A significant word used in an index as the first word of an entry.

Catchword Entry. An entry in a catalog, list, or index under a secondary part of the title as given on the title page, as a striking word or phrase that is likely to be remembered.

Catchword Index. An index with entries under a significant word or phrase.

Catchword Title. A partial title consisting of some striking word or phrase likely to be remembered by an enquirer.

"Categorical" Table. A list of forms and other qualifications applicable to any subject, with corresponding numbers, to be used for subdivision of topics in Brown's *Subject Classification.*

Cellulose Acetate. An acetate salt of cellulose that is used as a photographic film base. It is often called "safety film" since it is not readily combustible. [M.]

Cellulose Nitrate. Nitrated cellulose that is the main constituent of celluloid and is used as a photographic film base. It is highly inflammable. [M.]

Central Catalog. 1. The catalog of the central library of a library system. Also called Main Catalog or General Catalog. 2. A catalog in a central library of all the collections of a library system.

Central Library. The library which is the administrative center of a library system, where the principal collections are kept and handled. Also called Main Library.

Central Registration. A method of recording all borrowers in a union file at the central library whether borrowers' cards are issued at the central library or at a branch.

Central Shelf List. 1. A shelf list for the main library of a library system. Sometimes called Main Shelf List. 2. A combined shelf list for books in a main library and its branches or for a system of school libraries. Also called Union Shelf List.

Centralized Cataloging. 1. The preparation in one library or a central agency of catalogs for all the libraries of a system. 2. The preparation of catalog cards by one library or other agency which distributes them to libraries.

Cerif. *See* Serif.

Certification. The action taken by a legally authorized state body on the professional or technical qualifications of librarians and library workers in publicly supported libraries, based on standards adopted by the body, or similar action on a voluntary basis by a professional group such as a state library association.

Certified Bindery. A library bindery which has been approved as qualifying under the Certification Plan of the Joint Committee of the American Library Association and the Library Binding Institute.

Chafed. Having its surface worn by rubbing, as the cover of a book.

Chain Line. One of the parallel lines, usually about an inch apart, that appear in handmade or laid paper; produced in the process of manufacture. Running across the narrow way of the sheet of paper, chain lines are vertical in a folio book and in an octavo book, horizontal in a quarto book. Also called Chain Mark.

Chain Mark. *See* Chain Line.

Chain Stitch. *See* Kettle Stitch.

Chained Book. A book attached to a shelf or a reading desk by a chain to prevent theft.

Chalk Manner. *See* Crayon Manner.

Changed Title. A title used in a later edition or a reprint of a book, which differs from the title of the original edition.

Chapbook. 1. A small, cheap paperbound book containing usually some popular tale, legend, poem, or ballad, sold by hawkers or "chapmen" in the seventeenth and eighteenth centuries. 2. A modern pamphlet suggestive of this type of publication.

Chapter Heading or Head. A heading placed above the text at the beginning of a chapter.

Charge. A record of the loan of a book.

Charge Record (File material). *See* Out Guide.

Charge Slip. *See* Book Card.

Charging Department. *See* Circulation Department.

Charging Desk. *See* Circulation Desk.

Charging File. 1. A record of books loaned, usually consisting of book cards arranged by date or call number. Sometimes called Book Card File and Circulation File. 2. A charging tray.

Charging Guide. *See* Date Guide.

Charging Machine. A mechanical device for recording book loans. Also called Book Charging Machine.

Charging Slip. *See* Book Card.

Charging System. The method used in keeping a record of books loaned. Also called Loan System.

Charging Tray. A box for holding the record of books loaned. Also called Card Tray.

Charging Tray Guide. *See* Date Guide.

Chart. 1. A map especially designed to meet the requirements of navigators, showing soundings, currents, shoals, coastlines, ports, harbors, compass variations, etc. Charts include Portolan "maps." 2. A map exhibiting meteorological phenomena (barometric pressure, weather, climate, etc.) or magnetic variations. 3. A map of the heavens (star map). In collation, figures showing distances, dimensions, or motion of celestial bodies are considered diagrams. [Ca.]

Charter Hand. *See* Court Hand.

Chartulary. *See* Cartulary.

Chased Edges. *See* Goffered or Gauffered Edges.

Check List. 1. A comprehensive list of books, periodicals, or other material, with the minimum of description and annotation needed for identification of the works recorded. 2. A record of volumes and parts of serials or continuations received by a library.

Checklist Classification. *See* Documents Office Classification.

Chiaroscuro. 1. A system of printing engravings by the use of several blocks or plates to represent light and dark shades. The word means clear-obscure, that is, balanced light and shade. Also known as *Camaïeu* and *Claro obscuro*. 2. A print so produced.

Chief. (*a.*) A personnel rating term applied to a librarian in charge of a library or of a particular type of work, *e.g.*, chief librarian, chief cataloger. (*n.*) The head of a department or a division having a staff of two or more, *e.g.*, chief of reference department.

Chiffon Silk. A strong and durable silk material used for repairing and reinforcing paper, so sheer that the finest print is clearly legible through it.

Children's Book Week. *See* Book Week.

Children's Department. 1. The part of a library devoted to the reading of children. 2. The administrative unit of a public library system that has charge of work with children in the central children's room and all other agencies offering library service to children. Sometimes known as Junior Department and Juvenile Department.

Children's Librarian. 1. The librarian in charge of work with children in a department having a staff of less than two. *Cf.* Chief. 2. A professional assistant in a children's department assigned to one of the agencies in a library system giving service to children, usually a branch library or the central children's room.

Children's Library. A library devoted exclusively to service for children.

Children's Room. A room in the main building or in a branch of a public library set aside for service to children.

China Paper. *See* Chinese Paper.

Chinese Paper. A soft and very thin yellowish paper made in China from bamboo fiber and used for impressions of engravings. Same as India Proof Paper. Also called China Paper.

Chinese Style. Having pages printed on double leaves, *i.e.,* with unopened folds at the fore edges, and interior pages blank. The term Japanese Style is used when a Japanese book of the same type is described in cataloging. [Ca.]

Chrestomathy. A collection of extracts and choice pieces, especially from a foreign language, with notes of explanation and instruction. [By permission; from *The Century Dictionary and Cyclopedia*, copyright, 1895, by the Century Co.]

Chromatic Aberration. A distortion of an image by a lens that does not focus different-colored light in one plane. To the eye it looks like a rainbow at the edges of the image. [M.]

Chromolithography. A method of lithographic printing in colors by means of separate stones or plates for the various colors, with some colors printed over others. Also called Color Lithography.

Chronogram. A motto or inscription in which occur Roman numerals, often written as upper-case letters, that, added together or read in sequence, express a date.

Chronologic Filing System. A sub-arrangement of material according to date within any filing system.

Chronologic Order. An arrangement by date of copyright, imprint, or coverage, of subject cards in a catalog or of material itself; employed consistently under all subjects, or under such subjects as have a time element of significance, or for certain types of material, such as periodical articles or newspaper clippings.

Chrysography. 1. The art of writing in gold letters, as practiced by medieval writers of manuscripts. 2. Handwriting in gold, as in medieval manuscripts.

Chute. A sloping channel through which books or book containers may slide to a lower level. Also called Book Chute.

Circa. *Latin,* about. Prefixed to a date to indicate approximation.

Circuit Edges. *See* Divinity Edges (2).

Circulating Book. A book that may be taken from a library for use outside the building.

Circulating Library. 1. A library that lends books for use outside the library. The term is now used almost exclusively for a commercial rental library. 2. One of the small groups of books owned by a county school district and sent in rotation to the various schools of the district.

Circulation. 1. The activity of a library in lending books to borrowers and keeping records of the loans. 2. The total number of volumes, including pamphlets and periodicals, loaned during a given period for use outside the library. The term is used more commonly than its synonym, Issue.

Circulation Department. 1. The part of a library from which books for outside use are lent regularly to adults and young people. 2. The administrative unit in charge of all the routines connected with lending books for outside use to adults and young people. Also called Delivery Department, Issuing Department, Lending Department, Loan Department.

Circulation Desk. A counter or desk where books are issued and returned. Also called, according to division of the work, Charging Desk, Delivery Desk, Issue Desk, Lending Desk, Loan Desk, Discharging Desk, Receiving Desk, Return Desk, Slipping Desk.

Circulation File. *See* Charging File (1).

Circulation Record. 1. A record of books charged. Also called Loan Rec-

ord. 2. Statistics of the number of books charged daily for a given period. Also called Circulation Statistics. 3. The record on a book card of the number of times the book has been borrowed.

Circulation Statistics. *See* Circulation Record (2).

Citation. 1. A note of reference to a work from which a passage is quoted or to some source as authority for a statement or proposition. 2. Especially, in law books, a quotation from, or a reference to, statutes, decided cases, or other authorities.

Claro Obscuro. *See* Chiaroscuro.

Clasp. A metal fastening for a book or album; sometimes arranged with a lock.

Class. A division of a classification scheme under which are grouped subjects that have common characteristics.

Class "A" Library Binding. Library binding that meets the standards set forth in the Minimum Specifications as promulgated by the Joint Committee of the American Library Association and the Library Binding Institute.

Class Catalog. *See* Classed Catalog.

Class Entry. Listing a book in a catalog under the name of the class, that is, its general subject; in distinction from specific entry.

Class Heading. The word or phrase that designates a division in a systematic scheme of classification or in a classed catalog.

Class Letter. The letter used to designate a specific division of a classification scheme whose notation consists, wholly or in part, of the letters of the alphabet.

Class Librarian. *See* Classroom Librarian.

Class Mark. *See* Class Number (2).

Class Number. 1. A number used to designate a specific division of a classification scheme whose notation consists wholly or in part of numerals. Also called Classification Number. 2. The notation added to a book and to its entry in a catalog to show the class to which it belongs and indicate its location on the shelves of a library, in accordance with the classification scheme in use. Sometimes called Class Mark.

Class of Positions. A group of positions so nearly alike in character as to be designated by the same title and to require the same qualifications of personnel and the same schedule of compensation.

Classed Catalog. A catalog arranged by subject according to a systematic scheme of classification. Also called Class Catalog, Classified Catalog, Systematic Catalog, Classified Subject Catalog, and *Catalogue raisonné.*

Classic. 1. A work of such excellence that it is considered representative of the best in world literature, a national literature, or the literature of a sub-

ject. 2. *Pl.* Works of Greek and Latin authors.

Classification. 1. A systematic scheme for the arrangement of books and other material according to subject or form. 2. The assigning of books to their proper places in a system of classification. 3. In archives administration, the arrangement in logical order of the series or files within a record group or of the record groups within an archival collection.

Classification, Adjustable. *See* Adjustable Classification.

Classification, Decimal. *See* Decimal Classification.

Classification and Pay Plan for Library Positions. A recommended standard system of naming library positions in accordance with modern personnel terminology, and defining and grouping them through analysis of types of work performed and qualifications considered essential for each, with a definite scheme of promotion and schedule of compensation. Also, the written specifications and rules of administration for such a system.

Classification Chart. A synopsis of a classification scheme, designed to assist patrons in finding books in a library.

Classification Code. A formulation of principles and rules by which consistency may be maintained by the classifier in assigning books to their appropriate places in a system of classification.

Classification Décimale Universelle. A classification system based on the

Dewey Decimal Classification, expanded and modified by an international group of experts. Also known as the Brussels Classification.

Classification Number. *See* Class Number (1).

Classification of Libraries. A grouping or grading of libraries according to certain common characteristics or standards based on weighted criteria with point scores.

Classification Schedule. The printed scheme of a particular system of classification.

Classification System. A particular scheme of classification, such as the Decimal Classification and the Library of Congress Classification.

Classified Catalog. *See* Classed Catalog.

Classified Filing System. Arrangement by subjects in a logical sequence, usually indicated by numbers or symbols.

Classified Index. An index in which topics are grouped under broad subjects of which they form a part.

Classified Subject Catalog. *See* Classed Catalog.

Classified Subject Index. *See* Classified Index.

Classifier. A librarian who assigns books to their proper place in a system of classification.

Classroom Deposit. *See* Classroom Library (1).

Classroom Librarian. A student appointed to keep the books on deposit in a classroom library in order and to issue them to students, or to serve as a representative of the classroom in its relations with the school library. Sometimes called Class Librarian.

Classroom Library. 1. A semi-permanent or a temporary collection of books deposited in a schoolroom by a public or a school library. Also called Classroom Deposit, Grade Library, and Schoolroom Library. 2. A group of books from a college library sent to a classroom for use by instructors and students.

Classroom Loan. A small collection of books, usually material on a current school project, sent to a classroom for a limited period by a public or a school library.

Clay Tablet. An ancient Mesopotamian form of record inscribed in cuneiform writing on a piece of clay, varied in form.

Clearing House of Information. A term sometimes applied to a special library which has a limited amount of published material on file but gathers information by telephone and correspondence, and by the use of other libraries.

Clerical Assistant. A person who performs under supervision duties requiring experience, speed, accuracy, and clerical ability, but not knowledge of the theory of library work.

Cliché. A stereotype or electrotype plate.

Clientele. The borrowers and users of a library, as a whole. Specifically, the persons served by a special library.

Clipping Bureau. A commercial organization which clips articles on specific subjects from newspapers and magazines and forwards them to clients on a fee basis.

Clipping or Clippings File. A collection of clippings from current newspapers and periodicals, and other sources, arranged in some definite order in a vertical file. Also called Clipping Collection.

Clipping Service. A daily activity in many special organization libraries which includes clipping items of concern to the work of the organization, and sending them to officials, etc., of the organization.

Close Classification. 1. Arrangement of subjects in a classification system in minute subdivisions under inclusive divisions. 2. A method of classifying books that places them in minute subdivisions rather than in inclusive divisions of a classification scheme.

Close Score. The score of a musical work for three or more voices, in which the music is printed on two staves.

Closed Entry. An entry with completed bibliographical information covering all parts of a given work, viz., a complete set. [Ca.]

Closed Joint. The type of joint obtained when cover boards are laced on.

Opposed to French Joint. Also called Tight Joint.

Closed Reserve. A collection of books placed on reserve in a university, college, or high school library and only available to students through loans for short periods.

Closed Shelves. Library shelves not open to the public, or open to a limited group only, as in a college or university library. Also known as Closed Stack.

Closed Stack. *See* Closed Shelves.

Cloth. A generic term applied indiscriminately to the binding of any volume fully bound in cloth.

Cloth Sides. Having cloth as the side material, as in half, quarter, and three-quarter binding.

Clothbound. Bound in full cloth, with stiff boards.

Coated Paper. A very smooth paper produced by adding a composition of a mineral such as china clay and an adhesive to the original surface. Also known as Surface Paper and Enamelled Paper.

Co-author. *See* Joint Author.

Cockle. (*v.*) To wrinkle or pucker, from heat or humidity; said of paper and boards. (*n.*) A puckering effect of heat or humidity on paper or boards.

Code, Catalog. *See* Catalog Code.

Code, Filing. *See* Filing Code.

Codex. An ancient manuscript written on wax-covered tablets called codices; later, a manuscript on sheets of paper or vellum bound together like a book.

Coil Binding. *See* Spiral Binding.

Cole Size Card. A card devised by George Watson Cole for determining the sizes of books.

Collaborator. A person who works with one or more associates in writing a book.

Collate. 1. To ascertain, usually by examination of signatures, pages, leaves, and illustrations, whether or not a copy of a book is complete and perfect; also to compare it with descriptions of perfect or apparently perfect copies found in bibliographies. 2. To compare minutely, page for page, and line for line, in order to determine whether or not two books are identical copies or variants. [C.]

Collation. That part of the catalog entry which describes the work as a material object, enumerating its volumes, pages, size, etc., and the type and character of its illustrations. [Ca.]

Collation [by Signature]. A list of the signatures with indications of the number of leaves in the various gatherings.

Collected Documents. Annual or biennial reports of the various offices of a state collected annually or biennially in a bound volume under a collective title; *e.g.*, Connecticut Public Documents, Legislative Documents of New York State.

Collected Edition. An edition of an author's works previously published separately (sometimes by different publishers) issued in one volume or in several volumes in uniform style.

Collected Works. A complete, or nearly complete, collection of an author's published and unpublished works, issued by a publisher in one volume or in several uniform volumes, usually with an inclusive title.

Collection. A number of separate works or parts of works, not forming a treatise or monograph on a single subject, combined and issued together as a whole. [C.]

Collection (Archives). 1. An assemblage of record groups. 2. An assemblage of documents segregated from various record groups to facilitate preservation or servicing, as a map collection or a collection of indexes.

Collective Biography. A work (or, collectively, works) consisting of separate accounts of the lives of a number of persons.

Collective Title. An inclusive title for a publication containing several works, as the collected works of an author or a composer, a collection of an author's or a composer's works of a certain type; or an inclusive title for the several works issued in a series.

College Library. 1. A library forming an integral part of a college, organized and administered to meet the needs of its students and faculty. 2. In a university library system, a library with a collection of books related to the work of a particular college and administered separately by the college or as a part of the university library. 3. A library in a residential house at Yale serving one of the residential groups or colleges into which the undergraduate students are divided.

Collotype. 1. A planographic process of printing pictures similar to lithography, which produces accurate gradation of tone by the use of a gelatine-covered plate. Also called Photogelatine Process, Gelatine Process, and by the German term, *Lichtdruck*. Includes processes known as Albertype (or Alberttype), Aquatone, Artotype, Heliotype, Phototype. 2. A print made by this process.

Colon Abbreviations. Abbreviations for the most common forenames, formed of the initial followed by : for men and .. for women.

Colon Classification. A classification scheme prepared by S. A. Ranganathan which uses the colon to separate certain parts of a class number.

Colophon. A statement given in a book at the end of the text proper (frequently in early printed works though only occasionally in modern) giving some or all of the following particulars: the title or subject of the work, the name of the author, the name of the printer or the publisher (or both) and the place and date of printing. In addition there may be the device of the printer or the publisher, which alone would not constitute a colophon. [C.]

Colophon Date. The date given in the colophon. [C.]

Color-band Filing. An arrangement of books and pamphlets by means of colored bands pasted at varying heights across the backs to indicate an alphabetical, geographical, or other order.

Color-blind Film. Photographic film that is not sensitive to all colors. [M.]

"Color Books." A popular name for volumes containing documents and other material issued by governments in time of war or other crises to state their cases, each country using covers of a distinctive color, *e.g.,* the French Yellow Book, the German White Book.

Color Filter. *See* Filter. [M.]

Color Lithography. *See* Chromolithography.

Color Print. A print in more than one color, made either from one plate or block, or from two or more, as in Japanese wood-block prints. It may also be produced by the half-tone process, through the use of color filters, with successive printing of plates.

Color Sensitivity. *See* Sensitivity. [M.]

Color Slide. Usually, a single, mounted frame of a color film. [M.]

Column. One of two or more vertical sections of printed matter separated from each other by a rule or a blank space, as in newspapers and some books.

Column, Stack. *See* Stack Column.

Command Paper. A paper presented to the British Parliament by a department without a formal order of one of the Houses of Parliament, theoretically by command of the sovereign.

Commentary. A collection of explanatory or critical notes on a work, either issued independently or accompanying the text; *e.g.,* a commentary on the Bible.

Company File. *See* Corporation or Company File.

Company History File. *See* Organization (or Company) History File.

Compartment. A double-faced tier (*q.v.*).

Compass Map. *See* Portolan Chart.

Compendium or Compend. A work that presents in condensed form the principal points of a larger work; or, a work that treats a large subject briefly or in outline.

Compensation Guard. One of several short stubs bound in a volume to balance the space taken up by bulky inserts.

Competitor File. In business and other special libraries, a file containing information or material about companies and other organizations carrying on activities similar to those of the organization with which the library is connected.

Compilation. A work formed by gathering material from other books or writings.

Compiler. One who produces a work by collecting and putting together written or printed matter from the works of various authors. Also, one who chooses and combines into one work selections or quotations from one author. [C.]

Composite Volume. A bound volume made up of two or more· separately published works, such as pamphlets.

Composite Work. A treatise on a single subject produced through the collaboration of two or more authors, the contribution of each forming a distinct section or part of the complete work. [C.]

Compound Name. A name formed from two or more proper names, often connected by a hyphen, a conjunction, or a preposition. [C.]

Concealed Joint. A type of end-paper joint so constructed that the reinforcing fabric is concealed by the paper.

Concordance. An index of the principal words in the Bible or the works of an author, showing location in the text, generally giving context, and sometimes defining the words.

Condemned Book. *See* Banned Book; Index Librorum Prohibitorum.

Condenser. A large lens, or a system of two large lenses, used in a projector to collect and focus on the image to be projected the light from the light source. [M.]

Conditioning. The process of drying and sometimes hardening film after development. [M.]

Conference Room. A room set aside for the use of small groups when work with library materials is necessary to the development of an assignment or project. Found more frequently in school and college than in public liraries.

Confidential File. In a special organization library, a file of material which is segregated and used only under certain definite restrictions.

Congressional Documents. *See* Congressional Edition.

Congressional Edition. A special edition of United States Senate and House journals, reports, and documents, grouped in series and numbered consecutively, which Congress orders to be printed in this form after each Congress. Also known as Congressional Documents, Congressional Series, Congressional Set, Serial Set, Sheep-bound Set.

Congressional Series. *See* Congressional Edition.

Congressional Set. *See* Congressional Edition.

Conjugate Leaves. Two leaves which, when traced through the sewed fold, are found to form a continuous piece of paper. [C.]

Consideration File. A current temporary file of titles suggested for purchase, consisting of order cards, publishers' notices, etc.

Consolidated Index. A combined index to several volumes or a long run of a serial publication, or to several independent works or serial publications.

Consolidated or Union Trade Catalog. A compilation of data from several manufacturers in a single industry or group of allied industries; published for sale or rent by commercial publishers, or, more often, as an advertising venture, when it is usually free to certain libraries. Sometimes published by trade periodicals, either free to subscribers as a special or supplementary issue, or at an additional fee.

Conspectus. 1. A general survey of a subject. 2. A compact, systematic, sometimes tabular arrangement, as of items or facts.

Consultant. 1. A specialist in a particular subject associated with a library staff as adviser to staff and public, as in the Library of Congress. 2. A librarian acting as adviser to another librarian or to an institution in connection with special problems.

Consulting Librarian. *See* Consultant.

Contact Print. A print produced by having the sensitive film or paper in direct contact with the negative. [M.]

Contact Printing. A method for producing contact prints. [M.]

Contemporary Binding. A binding produced in the period of publication of a given book.

Contents. *See* Table of Contents.

Contents Book. A loose-leaf book listing contents of books, or titles of volumes or numbers of continuations and serials; sometimes used in place of listing on catalog cards.

Contents Note. A note in a catalog or a bibliography entry that lists the contents of a work.

Continuation. 1. A work issued as a supplement to one previously issued. 2. A part issued in continuance of a book, a serial, or a series. [C.]

Continuation Card. 1. A form used for ordering a continuation. 2. A form used for checking numbers of continuations as they are received. 3. An extension card (*q.v.*).

Continuation File. A list of serials, sets appearing at irregular intervals, and books in series, recording numbers and parts received.

Continuation Order. A general direction to an agent or publisher to supply until otherwise notified future numbers of a continuation as issued. Also called Standing Order.

Continuous Pagination. The numeration, in one continuous series, of the pages of two or more parts or volumes. [C.]

Continuous Printer. A machine for making film prints, in which the unexposed film and the negative pass in direct contact in front of a light source. [M.]

Continuous Re-registration. The renewal of registration of borrowers at various dates, as each borrower's registration period expires, rather than at a specified date for all borrowers.

Contour Line. A line on a map that represents an imaginary line on the earth's surface connecting points of the same elevation.

Contour Map. A map that shows elevations and depressions of the earth's surface by means of contour lines.

Contract System. The method by which a library in a city, town, or county makes a formal agreement to furnish library service to another community or group of communities.

Contrast. 1. The range of tones in a photographic negative or print expressed as the ratio of the extreme opacities or transparencies, or as the difference between the extreme densities. 2. The ability of a photographic material to differentiate between tones in the subject. [M.]

Conventional Title. *See* Uniform Title.

Conveyor, Book. *See* Book Conveyor.

Conveyor Capacity. The number of books a book conveyor is able to carry within a given period.

Conveyor Tray. A low, open box for carrying books on a book conveyor.

Cooperating Library. A library that joins another library or group of libraries in some common plan, such as limitation of its collections and service to a particular field, or contribution of cards to a union catalog.

Cooperative Book Buying. Joint purchasing of books and periodicals by two or more libraries in order to secure lower prices, or an arrangement by two or more libraries not to duplicate purchases of certain types of books.

Cooperative Book Selection. The policy adopted by two or more libraries of considering each other's holdings and selection of books before acquiring certain types of material, or special items, in order to avoid duplication.

Cooperative Cataloging. The production of catalog entries through the joint action of several libraries, in order to avoid duplication of effort. Particularly, the plan by which cooperating libraries prepare copy for catalog cards to be printed by the Library of Congress.

Copper Engraving. *See* Engraving; Line Engraving.

Copperplate Engraving. *See* Engraving; Line Engraving.

Copy. 1. A single specimen of a printed work. 2. One of the (theoretically) identical specimens of a work which together make up an edition, impression, or issue. Different copies may be printed on different qualities of paper; when printed in a different format they constitute different editions, *e.g.,* "large paper edition." [Ca.]

Copy Holder. *See* Book Carriage; Bookholder; and Copyboard. ([M.]

Copy Letter. A letter used to distinguish copies of titles having the same call number or having no call number.

Copy Number. 1. A figure used to distinguish copies of titles having the same call number or having no call number. 2. A number assigned to a particular copy of a book issued in a limited or a special edition.

Copy Slip. *See* Process Slip.

Copyboard. A platform on which material, usually flat sheets, is placed for filming. Also called Copy Holder. [M.]

Copyist. A person who transcribed manuscript books before, or at the same time as, the introduction of printing.

Copyright. The exclusive privilege of publishing and selling a work, granted by a government to an author, composer, artist, etc.

Copyright, Ad Interim. *See* Ad Interim Copyright.

Copyright Date. The date of copyright as given in the book, as a rule on the back of the title leaf. [C.]

Copyright Deposit. The free copies of a book or other work placed in a copyright office or designated libraries in accordance with the copyright laws of a country.

Copyright Notice. The statement concerning the copyright that appears in a copyrighted work.

Coranto. 1. An early seventeenth-century news sheet devoted to foreign news, appearing first in Holland and

Germany and in 1620-21 in England, issued irregularly and printed as a half-sheet in folio. 2. After 1622 in England, a quarto newsbook, usually appearing weekly and consisting of three sheets.

Cords. 1. Heavy hemp, cotton, or linen strings to which sections are sewed in the process of binding a book by hand. *Cf.* Tapes and Bands. 2. Heavy string reinforcements of the top and bottom edges of the backbone.

Corner. 1. The juncture of two edges of a book cover (usually the outer ones), or its covering. Various types are Square Corners, Round Corners, Library Corners, Dutch Corners, and Mitered Corners. 2. The leather or other material on the corners of book covers in half binding and three-quarter binding. 3. A cornerpiece (*q.v.*).

Corner Mark. Information added to the upper right hand corner of a catalog card to indicate language, editor, translator, etc., when there are many entries under the same heading.

Cornerpiece. A metallic or other guard used to protect the corners of books in shipping.

Corporate Body. A group of individuals associated together as an organized unit, *e.g.*, a government, a government department, a society, an institution, a convention, a committee.

Corporate Entry. An entry under the name of a society, institution, government department, bureau, or other organized body, for works issued in its name or by its authority, whether this be a main or an added heading. [C.]

Corporate Name. The official title by which a corporate body is known.

Corporation Card. *See* Business Firm Borrower's Card.

Corporation or Company File. In a special library, a file of material about the activities, securities, etc., of individual companies, such as annual reports and other publications issued by the corporations, stock exchange listings, prospectuses, clippings, etc. In a financial library the term "corporation file" is generally used; in other kinds of special libraries the term "company file" is sometimes used because it covers any type of business enterprise.

Corporation Library. 1. A library owned or controlled by a governing board legally constituted as a corporate body and including or not including municipal representatives. The library may or may not provide free public library service to its community. 2. A special library that serves a particular incorporated organization.

Correctoria. Medieval text forms of the Latin Vulgate used by copyists to secure correct copies of the original text.

Corrigenda. *See* Errata.

Cottage Binding. *See* Cottage Style.

Cottage Design. *See* Cottage Style.

Cottage Style. A seventeenth-century style of bookbinding in which the edges and bottoms of the cover were ornamented to resemble cottage gables. Also called Cottage Binding and Cottage Design.

Countermark. A secondary watermark in paper of the eighteenth century and earlier, recording generally initials of maker, place, and date. Its position is usually the center of the half sheet opposite that containing the principal watermark. The date watermark of the early nineteenth century is frequently placed near one margin.

Countersunk. In bookbinding, with a depression pressed or stamped to receive a label, an inlay, or the like.

County Library. A free public library maintained by county taxation for the use of the whole or a part of a county, established as an independent institution, or combined with a municipal or other library; or, a municipal or other library which provides library service to a county by contract.

Court Hand. A medieval cursive hand used in English court records, charters, and other official documents. Also called Charter Hand.

Cover. 1. The outer covering of a book or pamphlet, no matter what material may be employed. 2. Popularly, either of the two side pieces of a cover proper; as, front cover, back cover.

Cover (Periodicals). *See* Binder.

Cover Lining. *See* Inlay (1).

Cover Paper. Heavy durable paper used for making covers of booklets, pamphlets, etc.

Cover Pocket. A special adaptation of the inside of a book cover (usually the back cover) in which a pocket-like arrangement is provided as a receptacle for loose maps, and the like, accompanying the book. Sometimes called Pocket.

Cover Title. 1. The title printed on the original covers* of a book or pamphlet, or lettered or stamped on the publisher's binding, as distinguished from the title lettered on the cover of a particular copy by a binder. *Cf.* Binder's Title. 2. As restricted for use in collation, the title printed on the paper cover of a work issued without a title page. The paper cover is usually of different color and weight from the paper used for the text. [Ca.]

Covers Bound In. Original covers included, or to be included, in a later binding.

Cowhide. A strong, coarse leather which, when split, serves as the foundation for various types of leather.

Cradle Books. *See* Incunabula.

Crash. 1. Coarse, open-weave, starched cotton goods, used in edition binding for reinforcing backs of books. Also called "Super" and Gauze. 2. A pattern peculiar to buckram grades of book cloth, showing a coarse pebbled effect.

Crayon Manner. A method of etching by which the broken or dotted lines of crayon drawings are imitated through the use of various toothed wheels or disks called roulettes, and

---

*Unless qualified, a cover of any material, leather, cloth, boards, paper, etc.

other tools, instead of a needle. Also known as Chalk Manner.

Criblée. *See* Dotted Print.

Cropped. Trimmed unduly, sometimes so that the text is impaired.

Cross Reference. *See* Reference.

Cross Reference Sheet. A record in a vertical file, usually on a form sheet, of material filed under a different subject heading or in another file. In a special library it may refer to a particular publication, or a specific statement in a publication. It is sometimes used as a general reference between subject headings in a file.

Crushed Levant. A large-grained levant, with a smooth, polished surface, the result of having the natural grain crushed or polished down.

Crushed Morocco. Morocco in which the grain has been flattened by hand. Distinguished from Glazed Morocco.

Cubicle. *See* Carrel.

Cubook. A unit for measuring stack capacity; specifically, the volume of space required to shelve the average size book (average taking into account books of varying height and thickness) and allowing for vacant space 10 per cent of each shelf length. A cubook is a hundredth part of a standard section 3 ft. wide and 7½ ft. high.

Cum Licentia; Cum Privilegio. Having the right to print granted by authority. The phrase appears in sixteenth and seventeenth-century books.

Cumdach. An Irish term for a box, often elaborately decorated, for holding a bound or unbound medieval manuscript. Also known as Book Box and Book Shrine.

Cumulated Volume. The volume of a cumulative index or bibliography at the end of an annual or some longer period, which combines entries from earlier issues of the period.

Cumulative Index. An index in periodical form that at stated intervals combines new items and items in one or more earlier issues to form a new unified list; or, an index to any periodical that combines new entries with those of an earlier index.

Cuneiform Writing. The wedge-shaped writing of Assyrian and Babylonian inscriptions.

Curator. 1. A person in charge of a special collection, generally a scholar who can aid in the interpretation of the material. 2. A person who acts as honorary adviser in the selection and arrangement of material in special fields.

Curiosa. Books unusual in subject or treatment. The term is used for pornographic books.

Cursive. Having the letters joined together, as in early writing in private letters, documents, etc.

Curves. Curved marks ( ) enclosing inserted explanatory or qualifying words or phrases, or setting off some item in a catalog entry, such as a series note. To be distinguished from brackets [ ]. Also called Parentheses and Round Brackets.

Custodian. A person in charge of a building, a special collection, or some library agency, such as a deposit station or a traveling library.

Custom-bound. Bound according to the order of dealer or owner.

Cut. (*n.*) 1. A general term for an illustrative printing block, whether it be a line engraving, half tone, electrotype, or stereotype. 2. An impression from such a printing block. (*v.*) To trim the edges of books. (*a.*) Of a book, having cut edges. Not to be confused with Opened.

Cut Edges. The edges of a book when all three have been smoothly trimmed.

Cut Flush. Of a bound volume, having the cover trimmed after binding, so that its edges are even with the edges of the leaves. Also called Trimmed Flush.

Cut-in Heading. A heading at the side of a page in a rectangular space that displaces some of the text.

Cut-in Index. *See* Thumb Index.

Cut-in Note. A note at the side of a page in a rectangular space that displaces some of the text. Also called Cut-in Side Note, Let-in Note, and Incut Note.

Cut-in Side Note. *See* Cut-in Note.

Cut Out-of-boards. *See* Out of Boards.

Cutter Classification. *See* Expansive Classification.

Cutter Number. An author number from one of the Cutter tables or from the *Cutter-Sanborn 3-figure Alphabetic Table.*

Cutter-Sanborn Table. A three-figure alphabetical order scheme, an alteration of the two-figure Cutter table, made by Kate E. Sanborn. Also referred to as Author Table.

Cutter Table. Either one of two alphabetical order schemes devised by C. A. Cutter, consisting of decimal numbers so constructed that they may be combined with initial letter or letters of surnames or words, one table using two figures, the other, three figures. Also referred to as Author Table.

Cycle Stories. A series of tales selected from world epics and romance cycles, adapted for story-hour presentation.

Cyclopedia. *See* Encyclopedia.

Daily. A serial publication issued every day or with the omission of Sunday; as, a newspaper.

Data Compilation. In a special library, a regular recording of facts not assembled elsewhere, as information becomes available from day to day in miscellaneous publications; *e.g.*, a record of wage rate changes as reported currently by companies and industries, or a record of the discovered rates of corrosion of metals.

Date. *See* Accession Date; Binder's

Date; Colophon Date; Copyright Date; Imprint Date; Preface Date; Publication Date; Title-page Date.

Date Card. A card inserted in a book pocket to indicate date of issue or date when the book must be returned.

Date Due. The last day on which a book loaned by a library may be returned before a fine is charged.

Date Due Record. *See* Date Record.

Date File. *See* Date Record.

Date Guide. A guide marked with numerals for dates, used to arrange book cards in a charging tray. Also called Charging Guide and Charging Tray Guide.

Date Letter. *See* Biscoe Time Number.

Date of Issue. The day on which a book is charged to a borrower. Also called Date of Borrowing, Date Charged, and Date Loaned.

Date of Publication. *See* Publication Date.

Date Record. A record of books loaned, arranged by date of issue or date when books are due. Known also as Date File, or, if arranged by date when books are due, Date Due Record.

Date or Dating Slip. A strip of paper pasted on the inside cover or on the fly leaf of a book, on which is stamped date of issue or date when book is to be returned.

Date Table. In Brown's *Subject*

Classification, a table of letter combinations as symbols for dates.

Dating Slip. *See* Date or Dating Slip.

De Luxe Binding. A fine leather binding, lettered and tooled by hand. So-called de luxe bindings are often machine products.

De Luxe Edition. An edition characterized by superior materials and fine workmanship, usually a limited edition.

Decimal Classification. 1. The classification scheme for books devised by Melvil Dewey, which divides human knowledge into ten main classes, with further decimal division, using a notation of numbers. 2. An earlier variety of classification based on shelf arrangement rather than subject matter, in which tiers and shelves, each numbered from one to ten, were allotted to certain subjects.

Deck. The space occupied by one level of a stack, including ranges, aisles, elevators, and necessary working facilities.

Deck Area. The number of square feet on a stack deck, including aisles, range aisles, work space, and space occupied by stairs and elevators, but excluding carrels.

Deckle Edge. The rough, feathery edge of handmade paper, caused by a frame called the "deckle" used in molding the paper; or a similar edge in machine-made paper. Also called Feathered Edge.

Decorated Covers. In library binding,

bindings in which the front cover has an illustration, design, or special lettering.

Dedication. An author's note prefixed to a work, offering it to a friend or patron as a mark of esteem, affection, or gratitude, or as a plea for patronage.

Definition. The accurate concentration of light by a lens from one point in the object to the corresponding point in the image without diffusing the light in the image. [M.]

Definitive Edition. An edition of a work, or of the works of an author, presumably final as to text and, sometimes, as to annotations, commentary, etc. [By permission; from Webster's *New International Dictionary,* Second Edition, copyright, 1934, 1939, by G. & C. Merriam Co.]

Delinquent Borrower. A borrower who fails to return books, to pay fines, or to pay for lost books.

Delivery Department. *See* Circulation Department.

Delivery Desk. *See* Circulation Desk.

Delivery Station. A library agency without a book collection where borrowers can get books requested without going to the library, as material is sent there and returned at regular intervals. Also known as Call Station.

Demonstration Library. A library chosen or organized for an experimental purpose, in which a certain type of service is carried on during a specified period to prove the value of library service in an area.

Densitometer. An instrument for determining the density of a film. [M.]

Density. The measure of the degree of the opacity [of a film]. [M.] [By permission; from Webster's *New International Dictionary,* Second Edition, copyright, 1934, 1939, by G. & C. Merriam Co.]

Dentelle. A style of toothlike or lacelike ornamentation on fine bookbindings.

Department. 1. A major administrative unit of a library system set up to perform a definite function or set of related functions, and having its own staff and definite responsibilities, with a head directly responsible to the chief librarian or to the assistant chief librarian. 2. A section of a library devoted to a particular subject or group of subjects, as in a departmentalized library. Sometimes called Division.

Departmental Edition. An edition of the publications of the executive departments and independent establishments of the United States government, issued with no uniformity in contents, format, or binding, as distinguished from the Congressional edition, in which they are also issued as Senate and House Documents. Also called Plain Title Edition and, sometimes, Departmental Set.

Departmental Library. 1. A collection in a special field attached to a department of instruction in a college or a university, and administered as a branch of the main library or independently. 2. A library maintained by a government department.

Departmental Set. *See* Departmental Edition.

Departmental Shelf List. A shelf list of the books in a library department or in a departmental library in a college or university library system.

Departmentalized Library. 1. A library in which all books, periodicals, and pamphlets, whether for reference or circulation, are separated according to subject into several distinct divisions, as in a few large public libraries. 2. A college or university library that maintains separate but usually centrally controlled libraries for certain departments of instruction.

Deposit Copy. *See* Copyright Deposit.

Deposit Fee. Money deposited by a borrower who cannot qualify for a free card or who does not wish to ask for a guarantor, to be refunded when all books are returned.

Deposit Library. A library in which little-used books and other printed materials from a group of cooperating libraries are stored but are available on request. Also called Reservoir Library.

Deposit Station. A library agency in a store, school, factory, club, or other organization or institution, with a small and frequently changed collection of books, and open at certain designated times.

Depository Catalog. *See* Library of Congress Depository Catalog.

Depository Invoice. A list of the publications sent by the Superintendent of Documents to a depository library on a specified date.

Depository Library. A library legally designated to receive without charge copies of all or selected United States government publications; or a library designated to receive without charge a full set of Library of Congress printed cards.

Depth of Field. *See* Depth of Focus. [M.]

Depth of Focus. The distance over which the images of objects will be sharp. [M.]

Descender. 1. That part of a lower-case letter that extends below the body. 2. A lower-case letter with a part that extends below its body, as j, p.

Descriptive Cataloging. That phase of the process of cataloging which concerns itself with the identification and description of books.

Desiderata. *See* Want List (1).

Desk Schedule. An outline showing hours when staff members are assigned to duty in all departments serving the public.

Detached Copy. A copy whose pages have been actually removed from the work in which they were originally issued; usually applied to articles from periodicals.

Developer. A solution of chemicals for developing. [M.]

Developing. Chemically treating exposed photographic film to convert the latent image to a visible image. [M.]

Device. *See* Printer's or Publisher's Mark.

Dewey Decimal Classification. *See* Decimal Classification.

Diagram. 1. A linear figure which serves to illustrate a definition or a statement, or to aid in the proof of a proposition, as in logic, mathematics, or mechanics. 2. An illustrative figure which represents, in outline or general form only, the general plan or relative position of the parts of an object; *e.g.*, a working drawing or cross section of a scientific apparatus, a machine, an engineering or architectural detail, a piece of furniture, or a toy. Dimensions may or may not be given. 3.* A graphical delineation of relationship between persons, objects, etc., *e.g.*, an organization chart in education, business, or manufacturing; an efficiency chart showing arrangement of machinery or office furniture, or flow of materials or work; a schematic plan for heating, air conditioning, electric wiring, or plumbing; the plan of an athletic field or of the placing of equipment in a gymnasium; a plan for the arrangement of the instruments in an orchestra; a planting plan for a flower border. 4.* A graph showing by lines, bars, curves, surfaces, symbols, etc., the course or results of any action or process, or its variations; *e.g.*, the path of a moving body (for instance, the orbit of a heavenly body, the progress

---
* This type of diagram may be pictorial, *i.e.*, either illustrated or in the form of pictographs.

of plays or players in a game, the path of an actor on the stage); the fluctuation in temperature or barometric pressure; the variation or increase in population, land values, educational facilities, size. [Ca.]

Diaper. A small repeating pattern of binding ornament in geometrical form, usually a diamond or a lozenge.

Diaphragm. A device such as a perforated plate or an iris which limits either the aperture of the lens, or the field covered by the lens, or both the aperture and the field, depending on its location. Also known as Stops. [M.]

Diazotype Film. A film impregnated with light-sensitive dyes of the diazo group. This film is used for direct, contact printing, a positive being made from a positive or a negative from a negative. [M.]

Diced. Ornamented with crosslined tooling to resemble dice or small squares; said of calf and morocco.

Dictionary Catalog. A catalog, usually on cards, in which all the entries (author, title, subject, series, etc.) and their related references are arranged together in one general alphabet. The subarrangement frequently varies from the strictly alphabetical. [C.]

Diffusing Screen. A translucent screen that evenly diffuses transmitted light. [M.]

Digest. 1. A brief condensation of a written work, often in other words than those of the original. 2. In law, a compact summary of laws, reported cases, decisions, etc., systematically arranged.

Dime Novel. A story, usually of a romantic and sensational nature, published in cheap form and generally priced at ten cents a copy.

Diplomatics (Diplomatic). The study of official documents, usually early documents, including handwriting and chancery practices, for purposes of authentication.

Diptych. An ancient hinged writing tablet consisting of two tablets of wood, ivory, or metal covered with wax on the inside surfaces, on which writing was done with a stylus.

Direct Positive. A positive obtained on negative material by developing the latent image to a positive image, using a reversal process. [M.]

Direct Subdivision. Subdivision of subject headings by name of province, county, city, or other locality without intermediate subdivision by name of country or state.

Direction Word. *See* Catchword (2).

Director. 1. The chief executive head of a library or a library system. Also known as Librarian and Chief Librarian. 2. The chief administrative head of a library school, and occasionally, of a library commission. 3. Sometimes, a librarian in charge of a particular type of work in a library system, such as children's work, or a training class. 4. In a few libraries, the administrative head of one of the larger divisions, as in the Library of Congress. 5. A mem-

ber of the governing board of a library; a trustee. 6. In medieval manuscripts and printed books, a small letter placed in a space left blank for an initial, as a guide for the illuminator or rubricator.

Directory. A list of persons or organizations, systematically arranged, usually in alphabetic or classed order, giving address, affiliations, etc., for individuals, and address, officers, functions, and similar data for organizations.

Discard. A book officially withdrawn from a library collection because it is unfit for further use or is no longer needed.

Discharging. Canceling the loan record of a book when the book is returned to the library.

Discharging Desk. *See* Circulation Desk.

Discontinue Notice. A form used to inform a publisher that a serial received as a gift is no longer desired.

Disjoined Hand. A type of vertical handwriting with each letter separated as in printing. Sometimes called Printing Hand.

Display Case. 1. A floor rack with shelves for showing books, from which readers may select books. Also called Book Display Case. 2. An exhibition case (*q.v.*).

Display Rack. *See* Rack.

Display Type. Large and heavy-faced type used for headings, display lines in advertisements, etc., as distinguished from body type.

Dissertation, Academic. An essay or treatise presented by a candidate in partial fulfillment of the requirements for a degree. *Cf.* Program Dissertation. [C.]

Distributing Station. *See* Deposit Station.

District Library. *See* School District Library (1); Regional Library.

Divided Catalog. A card catalog separated for convenience in use into two or more units, as, an author and title catalog and a subject catalog.

Dividing Stroke. *See* Line Division Mark.

Divinity Calf. 1. A dark calf binding, with blind stamping and no gilding. 2. A binding leather used chiefly for the inside cover lining of well-bound limp-leather prayer books and small Bibles.

Divinity Circuit. Flexible binding, of soft leather, *e.g.,* seal or levant, with edges that extend over the leaves. Used principally for Bibles and prayer books. Also called Yapp, Box Edge, and Divinity Style.

Divinity Edges. 1. Red, or red-under-gold, book edges. 2. Overhanging limp-leather cover edges. Also called Circuit Edges.

Divinity Style. *See* Divinity Circuit.

Division. 1. A unit in a library system which is responsible for library service in a definite subject or related fields. 2. In some libraries, a department (*q.v.*). 3. In some libraries, a section of a department. 4. In a classification scheme, one of the groups into which knowledge is divided, whether a general class divided by sections and subsections or one of the subordinate sections or subsections. 5. In a classification scheme, a section immediately subordinate to a main class, as in the Decimal classification.

Division Library. A collection attached to, and administered by, a division or a group of related departments of a university or a college, usually with some form of cooperative arrangement with the general library or as a part of the library system.

Document. Any written, printed, or otherwise recorded item or physical object that may serve as evidence of a transaction. *See also* Government Publication.

Document Number. A number assigned to a government publication by which it may be identified. Particularly, in United States federal documents, the number of an individual document in one of the four series issued for each session of each Congress in the Congressional edition.

Documentation. The establishment, identification, collection, and use of documents.

Documents Office Classification. A scheme used in the Office of the Superintendent of Documents for the arrangement of federal government publications, based on the government author, *i.e.,* first by department or independent agency, then by bureaus, divisions, etc. Sometimes called Checklist Classification.

Dodger. A small handbill.

Dog-eared or Dogs'-eared. Having leaves turned down at the corners.

Door Checker. *See* Guard (Person).

Doorman. *See* Guard (Person).

Doric. *See* Sans-serif.

Dormitory Library. A library in a residence hall of a college or university, which provides students with recreational reading and, sometimes, reference books and books for required reading.

Dos-à-dos. A form of binding in which two books are bound together so as to open in opposite directions, one of the three boards used being common to both volumes, and with the two spines, and respectively, the fore edges, opposed.

Dotted Print. 1. A relief method of engraving in which the parts cut in relief print black, and half tones are obtained by punching small holes in the plate, which appear in the print as white dots on a black background. Also known as *Schrotblatt*, and *Manière criblée*. 2. A print produced in this manner.

Double-acting Card Catalog Case. A case for catalog cards, generally set in a partition, with double-ended drawers that pull out from either face of the case. Earlier called Double-faced Card Catalog Cabinet.

Double End Papers. End papers incorporated in duplicate in certain books. Each set, front and back, has two paste-down (pasted-down) and two end-paper fly leaves (free).

Double Entry. Entry in a catalog under two subject headings, one for subject and one for place, for subjects of local interest or for scientific subjects relating to a particular locality, *e.g.,* Birds—Ohio and Ohio—Birds. Also, entry of pseudonymous works under real name of author and, briefly, under pseudonym.

Double-entry Charging System. A method of recording book loans in which two records are kept, usually a time record and a book record.

Double Exposure. The exposure of all or part of the image area of the film in a camera twice in succession. [M.]

Double-faced Card Catalog Case. A cabinet made in one piece in the form of two catalog cases placed back to back.

Double Fold. A binding unit of a special kind of volume, in which a single-fold sheet serves as one leaf; the unopened fold becomes the fore edge, and the opposite free edges become the binding edge. The inner sides of the sheet are, of course, not used.

Double Image. Two photographic images of one object not exactly superimposed. [M.]

Double Leaf. 1. A leaf of double size with the center fold at the fore edge or the top edge of the book. 2. Any one of the two-leaf units composing a signature, gathering, or section.

Double Letter. *See* Ligature.

Double-perforate Film. Film that has perforations or sprocket holes on both edges. [M.]

Double Plate. A single unit of illustration extending across two confronting pages; often printed on a leaf of double size folded in the center and attached at the fold.

Double Slipcase. A slipcase in two parts, one of which fits into the other. Also called Telescope Box.

Double-spread Title Page. See Double Title Page (2).

Double Title Page. 1. A term used for two title pages that face each other, as in many German books; as a rule, one is for the series or set of volumes as a whole, the other for the particular volumes in the series or set. 2. As used in the book trade, a title page that occupies two facing pages. Also called Double-spread Title Page.

Doublure. The ornamental lining (frequently decorated) of leather, silk, vellum, or other material mounted on the inner face of the cover of a book. The doublure and its accompanying guard leaf take the place of a lining paper. [C.]

Doubtful Authorship. Authorship not proved, but ascribed to one or more authors without convincing evidence.

Drame à Clef. A play in which one or more characters are based on real persons, with names disguised.

Drop-down Title. *See* Caption Title.

Drop Folio. A page or folio number at the bottom of a page.

Dry Point. 1. A process of engraving with a sharp needle called the dry point directly on the bare metal without the use of a ground or acid as in etching. 2. A print produced by this method.

Dummy. 1. A piece of wood or some other material used to replace a book out of its regular position, on which is placed a label indicating the location of the book. 2. In a file or a catalog, a piece of paper or cardboard on which is indicated the location of material filed elsewhere or temporarily removed. 3. An unprinted or partially printed or sketched sample of a projected book, pamphlet, book cover, or other material to suggest the final appearance of the completed work.

Duodecimo. 1. Format: a book printed on sheets folded to make twelve leaves or twenty-four pages. 2. Size: according to the American Library Association scale, a book which measures 17.5 to 20 cm. in height. Also called Twelvemo.

Duplicate. An additional copy of a book already in a library, especially a copy to be disposed of by exchange or in some other way.

Duplicate Exchange. *See* Exchange (1).

Duplicate Negative. A negative printed from a positive, or from a negative by a reversal process. [M.]

Duplicate Pay Collection. *See* Rental Collection.

Duplicating Film. A film that gives a negative from a negative or a positive from a positive. [M.]

Dust Cover. *See* Book Jacket.

Dust Jacket. *See* Book Jacket.

Dust Wrapper. *See* Book Jacket.

Dutch Corner. *See* Library Corner.

Early Impression. *See* State (Engraving).

Early Sheets. *See* Advance Sheets (1).

Easy Book. A book for younger children, such as a picture book or a reader.

Eau-forte. *See* Etching.

Editio Princeps. *See* First Edition.

Edition. 1. All the impressions of a work printed at any time or times from one setting of type, including those printed from stereotype or electrotype plates from that setting (provided, however, that there is no substantial change in or addition to the text, or no change in make-up, format,* or character of the resulting book). A facsimile reproduction constitutes a different edition. 2. One of the successive forms in which a literary text is issued either by the author or by a subsequent editor.

* For a "large paper edition" (called also "large paper copy") the pages are usually, though not always, reimposed.

[Ca.] 3. One of the various printings of a newspaper for the same day, an issue published less often, as a weekly edition, or a special issue devoted to a particular subject, as an anniversary number. 4. In edition binding, all of the copies of a book or other publication produced and issued in uniform style. *Cf.* Textbook Edition, Trade Edition.

Edition (Old maps). The number of copies of a map which were printed by the same man, or men, at a given place and under a given publication date.

Edition Bindery. A bindery in which books are originally bound in quantity for publishers.

Edition Binding. The kind of bookbinding that is furnished to the book trade, *i.e.*, quantity binding in uniform style for a large number of copies of single titles. *Cf.* Publisher's Binding.

Editions File. A card list of editions which a library wishes to add to its collection or to duplicate.

Editor. One who prepares for publication a work or collection of works or articles not his own. The editorial labor may be limited to the preparation of the matter for the printer, or it may include supervision of the printing, revision (restitution) or elucidation of the text, and the addition of introduction, notes, and other critical matter. [C.]

Editor Reference. A reference in a catalog from an editor's name, or from an entry under the editor of a work to another entry where more complete information is to be found.

Electric Stylus. A sharp-pointed electrically heated instrument for impressing call numbers on books.

Electric Time Stamp. *See* Time Stamp.

Electrotype. A reproduction of a relief printing surface, made of copper, lead, or some other metal deposited by electrolysis on a mold of wax, lead, or a plastic, and backed with metal.

Elephant Folio. A large folio, about 14 by 23 inches.

Elephantine Book. A book recording acts of Roman officials, called elephantine because it consisted of ivory tablets.

Em. A unit of measurement in printing, being the square of the body height of any size of type.

Emblem Book. A type of book in which designs or pictures called emblems, expressing some thought or moral idea, were printed with accompanying proverbs, mottoes, or explanatory writing, or in which verses were arranged in symbolic shapes such as crosses.

Embossed Book. A book for the blind printed in raised characters.

Embossing. 1. The process of producing a design in relief on a surface by the use of a sunken die and a raised counterpart, as on leather. 2. Blind stamping (*q.v.*).

Embroidered Binding. A binding in which embroidered cloth is used as the covering material. Also known as Needlework Binding.

Employee Magazine. *See* House Organ.

Emulsion. A photochemically active layer consisting of light-sensitive chemicals in a very finely divided state held in suspension in a medium such as gelatine. The emulsion is supported on a base of paper, film, glass, etc. [M.]

En. In printing, half the width of a corresponding em but the same height. Used in England as a unit of type measurement.

Enamelled Paper. *See* Coated Paper.

Encyclopedia (Cyclopedia). A work containing informational articles on subjects in every field of knowledge, usually arranged in alphabetical order, or a similar work limited to a special field or subject.

End Leaf. The binder's leaf, of any material, which faces the lining of the cover. It may be either the free half of this lining, or a separate leaf sewed in with the adjoining signature. [C.]

End Papers. One or more leaves inserted by the binder at the beginning and the end of the book. End papers consist of the lining papers and any fly leaves which are not part of the printed signatures.* [C.]

---

* An outer blank leaf forming an integral part of a printed signature is sometimes used as a paste-down; therefore, a leaf missing from an end gathering need not necessarily have been a printed leaf.

End Sheets. *See* End Papers.

English Braille. Braille as adapted to the English language in contrast to braille adapted to other languages.

English-finish Paper. A calendered paper with a smooth but not glossy finish.

Engraved Title Page. As mentioned on the catalog card, usually an engraved title page which includes the title of the book within the decorative design or bears an illustration in addition to the title; it need not include the author's name or the imprint. [C.]

Engraving. 1. The art of preparing an incised design on a metal plate or a block of wood or other material, by cutting, the action of acid, photo-mechanical processes, etc., as the basis of impressions or prints. 2. A print produced by any of these methods.

Enlargement. A print produced by the process of enlarging. [M.]

Enlargement Ratio. The ratio, expressed in diameters, of the enlarged image to the original image. [M.]

Enlarger. A projector used in enlarging. [M.]

Enlarging. The process of producing a larger image of a negative or a positive by increasing the size of the image through projection on a sensitized surface. Also called Projection Printing. [M.]

Entry. A record of a book in a catalog or list. [C.]

Entry-a-line Index. An index in which each entry is brief enough to be printed on one line.

Entry Word. The word by which an entry is arranged in a catalog or a bibliography, usually the first word of the heading. Also called Filing Word. [Ca.]

Ephemera. 1. Current material, usually pamphlets and clippings, of temporary interest and value. 2. Similar material of the past which has acquired literary or historical significance.

Epigraph. An appropriate motto or brief quotation prefixed to a book or a chapter.

Epitome. 1. A concise statement of the chief points of a work. 2. A concise survey of a subject.

Erotica. Literature that has sexual love as its theme.

Errata. A list of typographical errors occurring in a book, with corrections, tipped in or laid in the book. Also known as Corrigenda.

Esparto. A grass grown in southern Spain and northern Africa, used in the manufacture of bulky lightweight book paper.

Essay Periodical. An eighteenth-century type of periodical, consisting usually of a single essay, as *The Tatler, The Spectator,* and *The Rambler.*

Etching. 1. A process by which a design is drawn on a metal plate with an etching needle through a waxy etching ground, then bitten with acid, and impressions taken from the incised lines. Also known by the French term, *Eau-forte*. 2. A print thus produced.

European Braille. Braille used in England and on the Continent, as distinguished from the now obsolete American braille. *Obsolete.*

Even Page. A page of a printed book bearing an even number, usually the verso of a leaf.

Ex Libris. "From the books," a phrase preceding the owner's name on a bookplate; hence, a bookplate.

Ex-library Copy. A dealer's description of a book once the property of a public or a circulating library, and therefore used or somewhat damaged.

Exact Size. The size of a book, generally its height, expressed in inches, centimeters, or millimeters rather than by fold symbol or size letter.

Exchange. 1. The arrangement by which a library sends to another library, institution, or society its own publications, or those of the institution with which it is connected, as a university, and receives in return publications of the other institution; or sends duplicate material from its collection to another library and receives other material in return. Also called, respectively, Publication Exchange and Duplicate Exchange. 2. A publication given or received through this arrangement.

Exchange Division or Department. The section of a library that handles exchanges.

Exchange of Librarians. An arrangement by which two libraries lend to each other simultaneously one or more staff members for a limited period.

Exhibit Rack. *See* Rack.

Exhibition Case. A glass-enclosed cabinet, sometimes built into a partition, or a showcase on a stand, in which books or other material are placed for display. Also called Display Case.

Expansive Classification. A classification for books prepared by C. A. Cutter, so called because in its series of seven complete classification schemes each one after the first is more minutely subdivided than the one preceding.

Explicit. A statement at the end of a manuscript or an early printed book noting its conclusion and sometimes giving the author's name and the title of the work. It is a contraction for *explicitus est,* "it is unfolded."

Exposure. 1. The amount of light admitted to a film, in terms of time and aperture. 2. The act of admitting light to a film. [M.] 3. The amount of an original which is microfilmed with one exposure (def. 2), usually two pages of an ordinary-sized volume; used as a basis for determining charges.

Exposure Meter. An instrument for measuring the amount of light available so that the time and aperture for an exposure can be determined. [M.]

Expurgated Edition. An edition from which objectionable parts in the original text have been deleted.

Extension Card. A catalog card that continues an entry from a preceding card. Sometimes known as Continuation Card.

Extension Library Service. 1. The supplying of books and other library assistance to individuals or organizations outside a library's regular service area. 2. In a university or college, the supplying of books and reference aid to organizations and individuals outside the campus by the general library or a library connected with an extension department. Also called Extension Service.

Extension Service. *See* Extension Library Service.

Extra Binding. The binding of books with more than ordinary care and handling, and/or with a higher quality of material, usually with ornamentation. Generally, binding in leather, but formerly, binding done by hand as distinguished from case binding.

Extra-illustrated. Illustrated by the insertion of engravings, pictures, variant title pages, etc., which were not issued as part of the volume or set. This additional matter, though often from other books, may consist of original drawings, manuscripts, etc. As a rule, it is mounted, inlaid, or trimmed to conform to the size of the book it illustrates. Synonyms: Privately illustrated; also Grangerized (a term derived from the vogue begun by the publication, in 1769, of James Grang-

er's *Biographical History of England* which had leaves left blank for the insertion of engraved portraits.) [C.]

"f" Number. The ratio of the focal length of a lens to the aperture. [M.]

Fabrikoid. The trade name for a brand of pyroxylin-coated cloth. The term is sometimes used generically.

Face. 1. The entire unbroken front of shelving on one side of a double case or on one side of a room or gallery. 2. The outside of the front cover of a book.

Face (Type). *See* Type Face.

Facetiae. 1. Witty sayings or writings. 2. Books distinguished by coarse and obscene wit.

Facsimile. As used in collation, an exact reproduction of manuscript or letterpress matter, or of music; usually made by lithography, photography, or some mechanical or photomechanical process. The facsimile need not reproduce the color or the size of the original. In a note, the term facsimile is used also to describe a facsimile binding or a facsimile of a medal set into the cover of a book. [Ca.]

Facsimile Catalog. A catalog which incorporates reproductions of slides, pictures, designs, etc., as part of the catalog entry for each.

Facsimile Reprint. In general, an exact reproduction of a printed work, whether from type or by a mechanical or a photomechanical process. Strictly, a type-facsimile (*q.v.*).

Facsimile Reproduction. A reproduction of a manuscript or printed work by means of a mechanical or a photomechanical process. [C.]

Fact Finding. *See* Research or Search Service.

Factual Book. In school libraries, an informational book interesting enough to be used for recreational reading, *e.g.,* a book on science, or a biography.

Fairy Tale. A traditional story that contains a supernatural element affecting human beings, animals, and inanimate objects. Also, a modern fanciful story of known authorship having similar characteristics.

"False First" Edition. An edition called "first edition" by the publisher when there has been a previous edition issued by another firm. [Ca.]

False Imprint. *See* Fictitious Imprint.

False Title. *See* Half Title (1).

Family Borrower's Card. A special card used in house-to-house rural service for charging to the head of a family books for the various members.

Fascicle (Fascicule). One of the temporary divisions of a work which, for convenience in printing or publication, is issued in small installments, usually incomplete in themselves, which do not necessarily coincide with the formal division into parts, etc. Usually the fascicles consist of quires, or of groups of plates, protected by temporary paper wrappers and may or may not be numbered or designated

as "part," "fascicule," "lieferung," etc. [C.]

Fatface (or Fat-faced Type). *See* Boldface (or Bold-faced Type).

Feathered Edge. *See* Deckle Edge.

Featherweight Paper. Very light, porous, bulky paper, usually made from esparto.

Fee Card. *See* Nonresident's Card.

Ferrotype. *See* Glossy Print. [M.]

Festschrift. A complimentary or memorial publication in the form of a collection of essays, addresses, or biographical, bibliographical, scientific, or other contributions, often embodying the results of research, issued in honor of a person, an institution, or a society, usually on the occasion of an anniversary celebration. [C.]

Fiber Cover. An extra-stiff but slightly flexible cover stock, used on large-sized pamphlet-like material.

Fiction. In popular library usage, narrative prose literature, with events, characters, and scenes wholly or partly the product of the imagination, as novels and short stories.

Fictitious Imprint. An imaginary imprint used for the purpose of evading legal and other restrictions, to mask piracies, to protect anonymity of the author, etc. Sometimes called False Imprint.

Fiddle. 1. To fasten leaves by winding a continuous cord through slots previously cut into the back edge of a book. 2. To fasten sections by means of a cross-stitch, the thread going from one section to the next and back again, down the length of the backbone.

Field Practice. *See* Field Work.

Field Representative. 1. A member of a local library staff whose work is to bring the library and its resources to the attention of the community. 2. A library organizer (*q.v.*).

Field Visitor. *See* Library Organizer.

Field Work. 1. The activities of a representative of a state library extension agency in direct contact with librarians and various groups, consisting of guidance in the administration of libraries and efforts to stimulate library development. 2. Actual work by a student in one or several libraries for a definite period as part of a library school course of study or a training course in a library. Also called Field Practice and Practice Work.

File. (*n.*) 1. A collection of cards, papers, or other material arranged systematically for reference or preservation. 2. A cabinet, case, or other device for keeping in order cards, papers, or other material. (*v.*) To arrange cards, papers, or other material systematically.

Filer. A person who arranges cards or other material in systematic order.

Filing Code. A body of rules for the systematic arrangement of cards in a catalog.

Filing Medium. The word, phrase, name, or symbol on a card or material to be filed that determines its place in a systematic arrangement. Sometimes called Filing Term or Filing Word.

Filing Term. *See* Filing Medium.

Filing Word. *See* Entry Word; Filing Medium.

Filler. The blank pages added at the back of a thin pamphlet when it is bound as a sizable volume. Also called Padding.

Fillet. A strip, or band, of gold leaf placed on a book cover, especially at top and bottom of the back.

Film. 1. A thin, transparent sheet or strip of material, usually cellulose nitrate or cellulose acetate, coated with a light-sensitive emulsion. 2. Either the base or the emulsion alone. [M.]

Film Advance. A mechanism for bringing film into position for exposure or for projection. [M.]

Film Edition. An edition of a printed work on film. Also called Film Issue. [M.]

Film Facsimile. A photographic facsimile on film. [M.]

Film Gate. A mechanism for holding film in position during exposure or projection. [M.]

Film Issue. *See* Film Edition. [M.]

Film Library. A collection of printed or manuscript material on films. [M.]

Film Projector. *See* Projector. [M.]

Film Size. The width of a film, usually expressed in millimeters. [M.]

Film Splicing. *See* Splicing. [M.]

Film Spool. *See* Reel (1). [M.]

Film Viewer. *See* Hand Viewer. [M.]

Filmslide. A length of film, usually a double frame, mounted for projection. [M.]

Filter. A piece of colored optical glass placed before a lens to remove certain wave lengths from the light entering the lens. Also called Color Filter and Light Filter. [M.]

Filter, Heat. *See* Heat Filter. [M.]

Finding List. A list of books giving very brief entries. If it includes books in various localities, it is sometimes called a Union Finding List.

Fine. A penalty for keeping books after they are due, in the form of a fixed charge of a few cents a day.

Fine Calculator. *See* Fine Computor.

Fine Computor. A device that indicates the amount of overdue fines to be charged a patron. Also called Fine Calculator.

Fine Slip. A slip bearing a record of fines charged a borrower for overdue books.

Finis. The end; frequently used at the end of a book.

Firm Card. *See* Business Firm Borrower's Card.

First Edition. The edition that is printed first. The terms Editio Princeps, Princeps Edition, and Princeps are generally used as synonyms, but are used by some bibliographers for the first printed editions of ancient authors.

"First" Indention. The distance from the left edge of a catalog card at which, according to predetermined rules, the author heading begins; on a standard ruled card, at the first vertical line. Also called Outer Indention and Author Indention. [Ca.]

First-line Index. An index to poetry, songs, or hymns, with entry under first line only.

First-word Entry. Entry made from the first word of a title not an article.

Fiscal Blue Book. A British government publication containing memoranda, statistical tables, and charts, with reference to British and foreign trade and industrial conditions.

Fist. *See* Index (2).

Fixed Book Collection. *See* Fixed Collection.

Fixed Collection. A collection of books sent from a central agency, such as a library commission or a central school system reservoir, which remains a unit wherever it is sent. Also known as Fixed Book Collection, Fixed Group, Fixed Group Collection; and, if for schools, as Fixed Classroom Collection, Fixed Unit.

Fixed Frame Camera. A camera that exposes single or double frames only. [M.]

Fixed Group or Fixed Group Collection. See Fixed Collection.

Fixed Location. The arrangement of books in a library by which each book is assigned to a definite position on a certain shelf. Contrasted with Relative Location. Also called Absolute Location.

Fixed Unit. See Fixed Collection.

Fixed Unit System. The sending of fixed collections to schools to remain for an extended period.

Fixer-hypo. See "Hypo." [M.]

Fixing. The chemical process of making a developed image permanent by removing the undeveloped light-sensitive substances. [M.]

Flange. The projection on either side of a rounded and backed volume. Also called Ridge or Shoulder.

Flap. 1. The projecting edge of a flexible book cover, as in divinity-circuit binding. 2. In the new-book trade, either of the two turned-in ends of a book jacket, on which the blurb and other data are usually printed.

Flat Back. A book back at right angles with the sides; opposed to the usual rounded back.

Flat Sewing or Stitching. See Side Stitching.

Flats. Two pieces of matched optical glass for holding film during projection. Also called Optical Flats. [M.]

Fleuron. See Floret.

Flexible Binding. 1. Any binding having other material than stiff boards in its cover. 2. Any binding that permits the book to open perfectly flat.

Flexible Classification. A classification scheme into which new subjects may be introduced without destroying the logical arrangement of the system.

Flexible Notation. A notation for a classification scheme that can be expanded with the growth of the scheme.

Floor Case. A double-faced bookcase standing on the floor of a room, detached from walls.

Floor Duty. An assignment away from the circulation desk to assist readers in selecting books or in finding particular books desired.

Floret. 1. Originally, a typographical ornament shaped like a leaf or a flower; now, any small ornament without a border line or frame. Also known as Flower, Printer's Flower, Type Ornament, and by the French term, Fleuron. 2. A leaf-shaped flower ornament used on bindings.

Flower. See Floret.

Fluid Unit System. See Block System.

Flush. See Cut Flush.

Fly Leaf. 1. A blank leaf at the beginning or the end of a book, between the lining paper and the first or last signature. 2. Loosely, also the blank free half of a lining paper or a blank leaf which is part of the first or last signature. [C.]

Fly Sheet. A single printed sheet smaller than folio, especially a handbill or a similar fugitive printed piece.

Fly Title. *See* Half Title (1).

Focal Length. The distance from the center of a lens of negligible thickness to the focal point when the object is at infinite distance. [M.]

Focal Point. The point at which a lens produces the smallest image of an object-point at a given distance. [M.]

Focus. (*n.*) See Focal Length and Focal Point. (*v.*) To adjust the position of the lens with relation to the surface upon which the image is formed so as to obtain the sharpest image of the object. [M.]

Fold Sewing. Book sewing done through the folds of signatures. Also called Sewing Through the Fold.

Fold Symbol. A symbol indicating the number of leaves into which a sheet is folded, and thereby approximately the size of the page, for example, 4°, 8°, etc.

Folded or Folding Book. A form of book consisting of a strip folded accordion fashion and attached at one or both ends to stiff covers. This type of book is common in the Orient and is less frequently found in other parts of the world, mostly in books of an unusual nature, generally pictorial, *e.g.,* views, panoramas, etc. [Ca.]

Folded Leaf. A leaf bound in at one edge but folded one or more times.

Folded Plate. *See* Folding Plate.

Folder. 1. A publication consisting of one sheet of paper folded into two or more leaves, but not stitched or cut. The pages of a two-leaf folder are in the same sequence as those of a book, but a folder of three or more leaves has its printed matter so imposed that when the sheet is unfolded the pages on one side of the paper follow one another consecutively. [C.] 2. A large sheet of heavy paper folded once, or with additional folds at the bottom, usually with a projecting tab at top of the back flap; used as a holder for loose papers, etc.

Folding Book. *See* Folded or Folding Book.

Folding Plate. A plate bound in by one edge and folded to fit the book, as distinguished from a double plate. Commonly called Folded Plate by catalogers.

Foliation. 1. The consecutive numbering of the folios (leaves) of a book or manuscript, as distinct from the numbering of the pages. 2. The total number of leaves, whether numbered or unnumbered, contained in a book or manuscript. [C.]

Folio. 1. Format: a book printed on full-size sheets folded medially once, making two leaves, or four pages. Also the form (proportions) resulting from such folding. 2. Size mark: according to the American Library Association scale, a book which measures over 30 cm. in height. 3. Foliation: an individual leaf or book, as folio 1, folio 2, etc., whether numbered or unnumbered. The number, if used, appears on the recto of the leaf. In early printed books the folio (leaf) usually has printing on both sides; the practice of numbering both sides as pages was not firmly established until the sixteenth century. [C.]

Folio Edition. An edition issued in folio form.

Folio Line. The line upon which the number of a page stands.

Folio Recto. *See* Recto.

Folio Verso. *See* Verso.

Follow Block. *See* Follower Block.

Follow-up File. *See* Tickler System.

Follower. *See* Follower Block.

Follower Block. A movable piece of wood or metal in a vertical file or card catalog drawer to hold material in an upright position. Also known as Follow Block and Follower.

Font. A complete assortment of type of one style and size, including upper- and lower-case letters, small capitals, punctuation marks, and special characters, with the necessary number of each.

Foot. The bottom edge of a book, opposite the head.

Footnote. A note at the bottom of a page bearing some relation to a particular part of the text above, as an explanation, or a citation of a source or authority, and connected with that part of the text by a corresponding number, letter, or symbol.

Fore Edge. The front or outer edge of a book; also called Front Edge.

Fore-edge Painting. A picture painted on the fore edge of a book.

Foreword. A preface; or, an introductory note in a book, in place of, or in addition to, a preface.

Form. 1. A blank or document to be filled in by the insertion of particulars. 2. A specimen document, blank, or record (including a sample catalog card) intended to serve as a model in framing others. [C.] 3. Pages of type metal and illustrations arranged in proper order for the printed sheet and locked in a metal frame called a "chase," ready for printing or for the making of an electrotype or a stereotype.

Form Card. A card used in catalogs that bears a printed or mimeographed statement applicable to many books, sets, headings, etc., with space for the addition of further information.

Form Classification. The classification of books that is based on the manner of presentation rather than the subject, as in the Decimal classification of literature and general works.

Form Division. A division of a classification schedule or of a subject heading based on form or arrangement of subject matter in books, as for dictionaries or periodicals.

Form Entry. An entry in a catalog which lists books according to (1) the form in which their subject material is organized, as periodicals, dictionaries, or (2) their literary form, as poetry, drama.

Form Heading. A heading used for a form entry in a catalog, *e.g.,* Encyclopedias and dictionaries, Periodicals, Short stories. Sometimes known as Form Subject Heading.

Form Subject Heading. *See* Form Heading.

Format. 1. In a strict sense, the number of times the original sheet* has been folded to form the leaves of the book, *e.g.,* folio (folded once, making two leaves); quarto (folded twice, making four leaves); octavo (folded four times, making eight leaves). Less strictly, the general proportions and approximate size of a book, etc., which would result from such folding. 2. Loosely, the general appearance and physical make-up of a book, etc., including proportions, size, quality and style of paper and binding, typographical design, margins, illustrations, etc. [Ca.]

Four-color Process. *See* Process Color Printing.

Foxing. The discoloring of paper by dull rusty patches, attributed to fungus, impurities in manufacture, dampness, or other causes.

Fraktur (Fractur, Fracture). Narrow
_____
* Paper is made in various sizes.

and pointed Gothic type with breaks or "fractures" in the lines, still in use in Germany.

Frame. 1. A binding ornamentation set in some distance from the edges of the sides. To be distinguished from Border. 2. The area of film that constitutes one exposure. The standard single frame is 24 x 18 mm.; the standard double frame is 24 x 36 mm. [M.]

Frame Line. The dividing line between two frames. [M.]

Free Access. *See* Open Shelves.

Free Reading. Reading done by students in school or college voluntarily, apart from any requirement by teachers. Known also as Voluntary Reading.

Free-reading Period. A class period when voluntary reading is allowed in a classroom or in a school library. Sometimes called Browsing Period.

French Guard. The back edge of an insert, turned over and folded around a signature.

French Joint. The free-swinging joint produced by setting the cover board a little distance away from the flange. Also called Open Joint. Opposed to Closed Joint.

Frequency. The intervals at which a serial is published, as weekly, monthly, annually, biennially.

Front Edge. *See* Fore Edge.

Front Matter. *See* Preliminary Matter.

Front Surface Mirror. A mirror that is silvered on the exposed surface. [M.]

Frontispiece. A leaf with illustration (other than an engraved title page) preceding the title page. The illustration usually faces the title page. A volume may be considered as having more than one frontispiece if two or more such leaves precede the title page, or if an additional frontispiece accompanies an added title page in an Oriental language at the end of the book. Ordinarily no other exceptions are made in cataloging. A frontispiece may be printed on one or both sides. [Ca.]

Fugitive Material. Material printed in limited quantities and usually of immediate interest only at the time of, or in the place of, publication, such as pamphlets, programs, and near-print material.

Full Binding. The binding of a, book completely, both back and sides, with any one material. Strictly, this term, and also the term "full-bound," should apply only to leather bindings. Also called Whole Binding. *Cf.* Half Binding, Quarter Binding, and Three-quarter Binding.

Full Cataloging. Cataloging that gives detailed bibliographical information in addition to the description essential for identifying books and locating them in a library.

Full Score. A score giving on separate staves all the parts of a musical composition to be performed simultaneously.

Galley Proof. A trial impression of type matter before it is made up into pages; named from "galley," a tray for holding type when it is set. Also known as Slip, Slip Proof, Proof in Slips, and simply Galley.

Gamma. The degree of contrast in a film. [M.]

Gap Card. A form card on which to record missing volumes and numbers of a periodical.

Gathering. 1. The process of collecting, and arranging in proper order, the printed sheets of a book or pamphlet, preparatory to binding. This assembling may take place before or after the sheets are folded. 2. The group of leaves formed by folding and laying together the one or more sheets or half-sheets which make up the signature. The term quire is preferred. [C.]

Gauffered Edges. *See* Goffered or Gauffered Edges.

Gauze. *See* Crash (1).

Gazette. 1. A newspaper. 2. Formerly, a journal containing current news. 3. A journal issued officially by a government; specifically, one of the official semi-weekly journals issued in London, Edinburgh, and Dublin, giving lists of appointments and other public notices.

Gazetteer. A geographical dictionary.

Gelatine Process. *See* Collotype (1).

Genealogical Table. A representation of the lineage of a person or persons in tabular or diagrammatic form. In cataloging, such representations of fictional families are designated genealogical tables, but graphic outlines of pedigrees of animals are considered diagrams. [Ca.]

General Catalog. *See* Central Catalog.

General Cross Reference. *See* General Reference.

General Information Reference Card. A card in a catalog referring from a specific subject on which the library has no books to a general subject which includes the specific subject.

General Library. 1. A library not limited to a particular field or special subject. 2. The main library of a university library system.

General Reference. A blanket reference in a catalog to the kind of heading under which one may expect to find entries for material on certain subjects or entries for particular kinds of names. Also called General Cross Reference and Information Entry.

General Secondary. In cataloging, a term sometimes applied to an added entry for a person or a corporate body whose relation to the work in hand cannot be indicated in the heading by the use of some specific designation such as editor, translator, illustrator, etc. [Ca.]

Geographic Division. Subdivision by country, region, or locality, as in a classification system, or in subject headings.

Geographic Filing Method. Arrangement of material according to place, alphabetically or by a geographic classification scheme. Sometimes, a subarrangement by place within any filing system.

Ghost. *See* Bibliographical Ghost.

Giftbook. An elaborate annual publication of prose and poetry, popular in the early part of the nineteenth century. Also known as Keepsake.

Gilt Edges. All three free edges of a book trimmed smooth and gilded.

Gilt Top. Having the top edge only trimmed smooth and gilded.

Glazed Morocco. Morocco in which the grain has been flattened by a calendering process. Distinguished from Crushed Morocco.

Gloss. 1. A marginal or interlinear note explaining a word or expression in a manuscript text. 2. A glossary (*q.v.*).

Glossary. A list of unusual, obsolete, dialectal, or technical terms, with definitions or explanations. Sometimes called Gloss.

Glossy Print. A paper print that has been dried on a metal or ferrotype plate. Also called Ferrotype. [M.]

Goatskin. Leather manufactured from the skins of goats; generally known as morocco or levant.

Goffered or Gauffered Edges. Edges decorated with a tooling or indented design after gilding. Also known as Chased Edges.

Gold Tooling. 1. Impressing an ornamental design in gilt on a book cover by means of heated "tools" (dies). 2. The effect thus produced.

Gothic. 1. Pertaining to a medieval style of handwriting distinguished by its angular character. 2. The style of type in the earliest printing of the fifteenth century, based on writing in medieval manuscripts. Also called Black Letter and Text. *See also* Sansserif.

Gouge Index. *See* Thumb Index.

Government Depository. *See* Depository Library.

Government Document. *See* Document; Government Publication.

Government Library. A library established in a government department or office.

Government Publication. Any printed or processed paper, book, periodical, pamphlet, or map, originating in, or printed with the imprint of, or at the expense and by the authority of, any office of a legally organized government. Often called Document, Government Document, and Public Document.

Grade Library. *See* Classroom Library (1).

Graded Scheme of Service. A system adopted by an individual library for classifying its employees according to types of position and qualifications required for each, with specified methods of appointment and promotion, and generally with a salary schedule.

Graded Service. *See* Graded Scheme of Service.

Graduate Library School. 1. A school for education in librarianship that met minimum standards of the Board of Education for Librarianship of the American Library Association from 1925 to 1933 by requiring for entrance a college degree, being connected with a degree-conferring institution, and meeting requirements with respect to faculty, curriculum, and other factors. *Cf.* Type I Library School, Type II Library School. Less exactly, a school for education in librarianship requiring a college degree for entrance. 2. The library school of the University of Chicago, which requires for admission an approved bachelor's degree or its equivalent, one year of training in a library school, and other requisites, and offers advanced work leading to the degrees of Master of Arts and Doctor of Philosophy.

Graduate Reading Room. A reading room in a university library for the use of advanced students, with a collection of special value for research.

Grain. Clumps of deposited silver in an image that show the structure of the image when the image is projected. [M.]

Grain Leather. The hair (or wool) portion of split leather.

Grange Library. A library maintained for its members by a local branch of the "Patrons of Husbandry."

Grangerized. *See* Extra-illustrated.

Graph. A representation of any sort of relationship by means of dots, lines, curves, etc., as in mathematics, chemistry, sociological and economic statistics, etc.

Gravure. Any intaglio process of printing an illustration from a design engraved or etched on a metal plate, as photogravure, rotogravure.

Green Film. Film that has not been sufficiently dried after development. [M.]

Green Paper. A popular name for one of a series of British government publications issued by the Public Relations Department of the Post Office dealing with the various aspects of Post Office work.

Groove. 1. A depression along each side of the back of a book, formed during the process of rounding-and-backing. 2. A depression along the binding edge of front and back covers. 3. The space between the board and the back of the book in an open joint.

Grotesque. *See* Sans-serif.

Guarantor. A person who identifies an applicant for a library card and assumes responsibility for his observance of library rules.

Guarantor's Card. A form signed by a guarantor.

Guard (Binding). 1. A strip of paper, muslin, or other thin material, on which an insert, leaf, section, or map may be fastened to permit free flexing.

Also called Stub. 2. One of several strips of paper or fabric put together to balance the space to be taken up by a folded insert. 3. A strip of paper or other material reinforcing a signature. 4. A guard leaf (*q.v.*).

Guard (Person). A man stationed to control a library exit, to see that library material to be taken from the building is properly charged, and to perform various other duties, such as checking parcels and wraps. Also called Doorman and Door Checker.

Guard Leaf or Guard. An end leaf faced with silk or other material to protect and complement the doublure which it accompanies. [C.]

Guard Sheet. As used on the catalog card, a leaf of paper (usually thinner than that on which the remainder of the book is printed) bearing descriptive letterpress or an outline drawing, inserted to protect and elucidate the plate or illustration which it accompanies. The guard sheet is not normally included in the pagination. If the descriptive letterpress is printed on the same kind of paper as the remainder of the book, the term leaf may be used. [C.]

Guarded Signatures. Signatures, usually the first and the last of a volume, that have cambric pasted around the back to condition them for sewing.

Guide. A card, or a sheet of metal, having a projecting labelled edge or tab higher than the material with which it is used, inserted in a file to indicate arrangement and aid in locating material in the file. For a card the term Guide Card is also used.

Guide, Out. *See* Out Guide.

Guide Card. *See* Guide.

Guide Slip. *See* Process Slip.

Guide Word. *See* Catchword (2).

Guidebook. A handbook for travelers that gives information about a city, region, or country, or a similar handbook about a building, museum, etc.

Guinea Edge. On book cover edges, a pattern resembling the milled edge of a gold guinea.

Gutter. The combined marginal space formed by the two inner margins of confronting pages of a book.

Gypsographic Print. *See* Seal Print.

Hachure. On a map, one of a group of lines of varying length and thickness that represent the direction and steepness of slopes on the surface of the earth.

Halation. The reflection of light from the back surface of a bright spot on a film to the surrounding darker portions, for example, the halo around a street light in a night picture. [M.]

Half Binding. A style of hand binding having a leather back, leather corners, and cloth or paper sides. In this style of binding the leather of the back usually extends on the boards one-quarter the width of the board, and the corners are in harmonious proportion. The term is applied also to any similar combination of two different materials. There is a current tendency to consider half binding as not having leather corners.

Half Leather. A half binding in which the back and corners are of leather, and the sides of some different material; *e.g.,* half roan, half morocco, etc.

Half Linen. A style of edition binding in which the back of the volume is covered with linen, and the sides usually with paper.

Half Title. 1. A brief title (of a book, a series, or a collection) without imprint and usually without the author's name, printed on a separate leaf preceding the main title page. Called also Fly Title, Bastard Title, and False Title. 2. A brief title, printed on a separate leaf or page, preceding the text or introducing the sections of a work. Although the brief title printed at the beginning of the first page of text is sometimes called the half title, the term caption title is to be preferred. The half title introducing a section of a work is called also Section Title and Sectional Title. 3. By extension, the page or leaf bearing the half title, although strictly these should be called half-title page and half-title leaf. [C.]

Half Tone. 1. A photoengraving plate on which a picture with gradations of tone has been photographed through a glass screen with fine cross rulings that break up the tones into dots. Also known as Half-tone Plate and Half-tone Block. 2. A print or an illustration produced from a half-tone plate.

Half-tone Paper. A supercalendered or coated paper used for printing half tones.

Half-uncial. Relating to a medieval type of handwriting that combined uncial and minuscule forms.

Hall Braille Writer. An obsolete machine for writing braille invented by Frank H. Hall in 1892. *Cf.* Braille writing machine.

Hand-copied Book. A book for the blind in which the braille transcribing has been done by hand on a braille tablet or a braille machine. Only one copy can be made at a time.

Hand List. A reference list in convenient form.

Hand Tooling. *See* Tooling.

Hand Viewer. A simple, monocular optical device for reading short lengths of microfilm of low or medium minification. Also called Film Viewer and Viewer. [M.]

Handbill. A small sheet containing an advertisement, to be distributed by hand.

Handbook. A small reference book; a manual.

Handmade Paper. Paper made by dipping a fine screen mold into the paper pulp by hand and lifting it with a peculiar motion that forms the sheet.

Hanging Indention. Specifically, a form of indention in cataloging in which the first line begins at author indention, and succeeding lines at title indention. [Ca.]

Hanging Press. *See* Rolling Press.

Hard-grained Morocco. Morocco in which the natural network grain has been stretched in two directions. *Cf.* Straight-grained Morocco.

Hardener. A solution of chemicals that hardens the gelatine of the emulsion and renders it insoluble and resistant to scratches. [M.]

Head. 1. (*a.*) A personnel rating term applied to a librarian in charge of a library, or of a particular type of work; *e.g.*, head librarian, head cataloger. (*n.*) A librarian in charge of a department, division, etc.; *e.g.*, head of branch department, head of technology division. 2. The top of a book or a page. 3. By extension, the top portion of the backbone of a bound book.

Head Title. *See* Caption Title.

Headband. A small ornamental, and sometimes protective, band, generally of mercerized cotton or silk, placed at the head and tail of a book between the cover and the backs of the folded signatures. Formerly the two were distinguished as "headband" and "tailband"; now both are called "headbands."

Heading. 1. The word or words at the top of a page, chapter, section, or article. 2. In cataloging, the word, name, or phrase at the head of an entry to indicate some special aspect of the book (authorship, subject content, series, title, etc.) and thereby to bring together in the catalog associated and allied material. [Ca. (def. 2).]

Headline. 1. The line at the top of

the page giving the title of the book or the subject of the chapter or of the page. The headline of a single page is called also Pagehead. *Cf.* Running Title, Caption. [C.] 2. One of the lines above a newspaper item or article indicating the subject in concise and generally striking form.

Headpiece. An ornamental design at the top of a page or at the beginning of a chapter.

Hearings. United States government publications in which are printed transcripts of testimony given before the various committees of Congress.

Heat Filter. Usually, a thick piece of plate glass placed between the light source and the condenser in a projector to remove much of the heat from the light falling on the film. [M.]

Heat Screen. A wire screen used as a heat filter. [M.]

Heliotype. *See* Collotype (1).

Hieroglyphics. Ancient Egyptian picture writing; also picture writing of any people, as that of the Aztecs.

Hinge. 1. Any paper or muslin stub, or guard, that permits the free flexing of an insert, leaf, section, or map. 2. Joint (def. 1) (*q.v.*).

History Card. A card in a catalog under the name of a corporate body that states briefly the date of founding, date of incorporation, change of name, and affiliation or union with other bodies. Sometimes called Information Card.

Holdings. 1. The books, periodicals, and other material in the possession of a library. 2. Specifically, the volumes or parts of a serial in the possession of a library.

Hollow. The open space between the cover and the book back of a looseback volume.

Hollow Back. *See* Loose Back.

Holograph. A manuscript or document wholly in the author's own handwriting.

Home Library. An early form of traveling library sent to a home by a city library or a library extension agency. Also called House Library.

Home Library Visitor. A staff member delegated to make personal contact with groups served by small collections of books placed in a home. *Obsolescent.*

Home Use. The use of library books outside the library, and sometimes, in recording circulation, the use of books loaned from a traveling library.

Hornbook. An early form of primer, consisting of a sheet of parchment or paper, mounted on a thin piece of wood with a handle at the bottom and protected by transparent horn. *Cf.* Battledore.

Hospital Library. 1. A library maintained by a hospital for the use of its staff, or its staff and patients. 2. A collection of books sent to a hospital from a public library for the use of the patients.

Hot Spot. A bright spot in the center of a projected image. [M.]

House Library. 1. A home library (*q.v.*). 2. A library in a residential house at Harvard serving one of the residential groups or houses into which the undergraduate students are divided.

House Organ. A type of periodical issued by companies and other organizations for: (1) internal distribution, *i.e.*, to employees; often largely concerned with personal and personnel matters; sometimes called Employee Magazine or Plant Publication; (2) for external distribution, *i.e.*, to dealers, customers, and potential customers; generally including articles on the company's products and on subjects related to the industry.

Humanistic Hand. A medieval handwriting less angular than Gothic, based on old Roman capitals and the Carolingian minuscule.

Hygrometer. An instrument for measuring humidity. [M.]

"Hypo." Sodium thiosulphate, the fixing agent almost invariably used to remove any undeveloped light-sensitive substances from film. Also called Fixer-hypo. [M.]

I Size Card. *See* Index Size Card.

Iconography. The study of the pictorial representation of persons or objects in portraits, statues, coins, etc.

Identification Card. A card issued to a borrower, bearing his name, address, and registration number.

Identification Number. A number stamped in a book, pamphlet, or other material as a substitute for other accession records.

Identification Strip. A short strip of film at the beginning of a roll of microfilm, on which has been photographed a description of the film, in letters large enough to be read with the naked eye. [M.]

Ideograph or Ideogram. A symbol or picture used in writing to represent an object or an idea, as in hieroglyphics.

Illuminated. Adorned by hand with richly colored ornamental initial letters, decorative designs, or illustrations.

Illustrated Covers. *See* Decorated Covers.

Illustration. A pictorial or other representation in or belonging to a book or other publication, as issued; usually designed to elucidate the text. In the narrow sense the term stands for illustrations within the text (*i.e.*, those which form part of the text page, or which are printed on a leaf bearing, on the reverse side, text other than mere descriptive legend). Normally such illustrations are included in the pagination. [Ca.]

Illustrator. An artist who draws the pictorial illustrations for a book or periodical.

Image. 1. A reproduction of an object, formed by a lens or a mirror. 2. A photographic image is the deposit of silver that forms the picture. [M.]

Image, Latent. *See* Latent Image. [M.]

Imitation Russia. Vegetable-tanned leather finished with oil of crude birch to give it the odor characteristic of genuine russia.

Impression (Binding). The effect produced by stamping, printing, or tooling a design or lettering on the cover of a volume.

Impression (Edition, etc.). All copies of a work printed at one time from one setting of type. There may be several impressions, presumably unaltered, of one edition, each new printing from standing type or original plates constituting a "new impression" of the work. Sometimes called Printing. If, however, the pages are reimposed to produce a different format, the resultant impression should be considered a different edition. For "revised (or corrected) impression," *see* Issue (Edition, etc.). [Ca.].

Impression (Engravings and old maps). A single copy of a print or map.

Imprimatur. In old books, a statement of official permission to publish given by a secular or an ecclesiastical authority. The term is now found chiefly in religious works by Catholic authors.

Imprint. 1. The place and date of publication, and the name of the publisher or the printer (or sometimes both); ordinarily printed at the foot of the title page. Originally the term applied only to the printer's imprint, which consisted of his name and place of business. Later the term was extended to include the name of the publisher and the place and date of publication. The printer's name, with or without address, is now more often printed inconspicuously on the verso of the title leaf or at the foot of the last printed page of the final signature. 2. The statement giving such information in a bibliographical description of a printed work. [Ca.] 3. A book or other publication that has been printed. The term is often used for a book printed in a· particular country or place, as "early American imprint."

Imprint (Binding). 1. The name of the owner of a book as stamped on the binding, usually at bottom of the spine. Also known as Library Stamp. 2. The name of the publisher as stamped on the publisher's binding, usually at bottom of the spine. 3. The name of the binder as stamped on the cover. (Not used by library binders in the United States.)

Imprint Date. The year of publication or printing as specified on the title page. [C.]

In Boards. An obsolete style of binding in which the book was trimmed after the board sides had been laced onto the bound volume. Short for "cut in boards." Not to be confused with Boards.

In Press. In process of being printed.

In Print. Available from the publisher.

In Progress. Not complete, but with

volumes or parts issued as they are ready.

In Quires. Said of a book in folded sheets, not stitched or bound. Also spoken of as "in sheets," or "in signatures." "In quires" is preferred because of its connotation that the sheets have been folded. [Ca.]

In Sheets. Said of a book, with printed sheets not folded, or with printed sheets folded but not stitched or bound. For the latter state "in quires" is preferred. [Ca.]

In Signatures. *See* In Quires.

In the Trade. Issued by and obtainable from regular publishing firms rather than from government or private presses.

Incipit. "Here begins." The opening words of a medieval manuscript or an early printed book, or of one of its divisions; if at the beginning, often introducing name of the author and title of the work, and sometimes called Title Caption.

Inclusive Edition. An edition of all of an author's works, or all of a particular type, written or published up to the time of its publication.

Incomplete File. A periodical or newspaper set from which volumes or numbers are lacking. Also called Broken File.

Incunabula (Incunables). (From the Latin, pl., *cunabula,* cradle.) Books printed from movable type during the fifteenth century. Also known as Cradle Books.

Incut Note. *See* Cut-in Note.

Indention. Specifically, the distance from the left edge of a catalog card at which, according to predetermined rules, the various parts of the description and their subsequent lines begin. [Ca.]

Independent. One of two or more pamphlets or bibliographically independent books, not sequents, bound together after publication. Sometimes called informally in cataloging a "Bound with."

Index. 1. A list of topics, names, etc., treated in a book or a group of books, with references to pages where they occur. 2. A card list in a library of references to material on a special topic, subject, etc. 3. A guide to material arranged by a different scheme from that used for the material itself, *e.g.,* a list in a special library by trade name of material filed by name of company. 4. In a special library, a list of special sources of information not in the library. 5. The character ☞, an old style reference mark, used to point to material. Also known as a Hand, a Fist, or an Index Finger. 6. A shortened form for the *Index Librorum Prohibitorum.*

Index Librorum Prohibitorum. The list of books which Catholics are forbidden by the highest ecclesiastical authority to read or retain without authorization. Commonly called the Index, and the Roman Index. Also known as Index Purgatorius.

Index Map. A key map that shows the location of the various areas represented by single maps when a group of maps has been prepared, or is being prepared, on the same scale for sections of a larger area. Also called Location Map.

Index Purgatorius. *See* Index Librorum Prohibitorum.

Index Size Card. A card 12.5 x 7 centimeters, formerly used for library records. Also known as I Size Card.

Indexing Service. Indexes, frequently cumulative, for particular subjects or for certain types of publications, supplied by an agency regularly through subscription or in response to special requests.

India Paper. A strong, very thin opaque paper made to resemble Oriental paper; used for Bibles and some reference books. Also known as Bible Paper.

India Proof Paper. *See* Chinese Paper.

Indicator. 1. A board on which is flashed the number of a ticket given to a reader waiting for a book requested, to show that his book is ready. 2. A device used in English libraries, and sometimes in American libraries in the past, to show whether a book desired is on the shelf or in circulation.

Indirect Subdivision. Subdivision of subject headings by name of country or state with further subdivision by name of province, county, city, or other locality.

Information Card. *See* Authority Card; History Card.

Information Desk. A desk or a table in the charge of an assistant who directs readers to the various parts of the library building and assists them with general information.

Information Entry. *See* General Reference.

Information File. 1. A file containing pamphlets and other material useful for miscellaneous information, arranged for ready reference. 2. A card file of references to sources of information on various topics.

Infra-red Light. Light that is not visible to the naked eye because its wave length is longer than that of the deepest visible red light. [M.]

Initial Letter. A large capital letter, often ornamental in design, at beginning of the first word of a chapter or paragraph. Also called Ornamental Initial and Initial.

Inlaid. 1. Inset in a border or frame of paper, the overlapping edges first having been shaved thin in order to make the resultant sheet of uniform thickness. A remargined leaf is not necessarily inlaid. 2. Laid between the halves of a paper or cardboard mat which protects and enframes. [C.] 3. The condition of a leather-bound book in which the cover has had another color or kind of leather set in.

Inlay. 1. In library binding, the paper used for stiffening the backbone of the cover. Commonly, but less strictly, called Back Lining or Backstrip. 2. A picture or decoration inserted in a book cover by inlaying.

Cf. Onlay. 3. A piece of graphic material, like a manuscript or a letter, mounted in a cutout frame of paper so that both sides can be seen.

Inner Indention. *See* "Second" Indention.

Inner Margin. *See* Back Margin.

Inscribed Copy. A copy of a book in which has been written a person's name, remarks, or both a name and remarks, especially one with autograph of the author.

Insert. 1. An illustration, map, or other piece, produced separately from the body of a book, but bound in it. 2. In newspapers and magazines, and sometimes other publications, an extraneous piece, not originally an integral part of a publication, slipped in to accompany the publication.

In-service Training. A program of systematic instruction and practice provided, planned, and organized by a library administration to aid in the professional development of staff members while they are engaged in their work.

Inset. 1. A smaller map, illustration, etc., printed within the border of a larger one. 2. The folded offcut, inserted at the center of the quire in some formats, *e.g.*, in duodecimo, etc. *Cf.* Offcut, Signature. [Ca.]

Inset Map. A smaller map printed within the border of a larger one. Not to be confused with a continuation of a larger map printed within the same border. [Ca.]

Inside Margin. 1. The back margin (*q.v.*). 2. The part of the turn-in on a book cover not covered by the end paper.

Inside Strip. *See* Joint (1).

Inspector of Libraries. *See* Library Organizer.

Institutional Library. A library maintained by a public or a private institution, as a prison library, a hospital library.

Intaglio Printing or Intaglio. Printing from a design cut into or etched on a surface, usually of metal, the incised lines holding the ink; *e.g.*, engraving, photogravure. Contrasted with relief printing and lithographic printing.

Interbranch Loan. A loan of material by one branch library to another.

Interbranch Record. A union list at a central library of all borrowers in the library system, with addresses, notes of unpaid fines, and similar information.

Interchange of Librarians. *See* Exchange of Librarians.

Interests Record. A record indicating the work interests of individuals among a special library's clientele, as a guide to the library staff for abstracting, routing, etc.

Interim Copyright. *See* Ad Interim Copyright.

Interleaved. Having leaves, usually

blank leaves, inserted between the ordinary leaves.

Interlibrary Loan. 1. A cooperative arrangement among libraries by which one library may borrow material from another library. 2. A loan of library material by one library to another library.

Interlinear. 1. Between the lines of a text, as interlinear notes. 2. Written or printed with explanatory notes, translation, or glosses between the lines of the text.

Intermediate Department. *See* Young People's Department.

Intern. A professionally trained young librarian who is working in a library for a specified period in order to receive planned and supervised training that allows the application of theory to actual, varied practice.

International Copyright. A system of common copyright privilege accorded to authors, composers, and artists in those countries that are members of the International Copyright Union under the Berne Convention of 1886 and the Berlin Convention of 1908.

Introduction. A preliminary part of a book that states the subject and discusses the treatment of the subject in the book.

Introduction Date. The date of a book as given at the beginning or at the end of the introduction.

Inventory. 1. A checking of the book collection of a library with the shelf list record to discover books missing from shelves. 2. In archives administration, a list of the material in a record group arranged basically in the order in which the material is arranged.

Inventory Truck. A small movable desk-like truck, fitted to hold a card tray and with space for books, for use in inventory.

Inverted Heading. A subject heading with the natural order of the words transposed, *e.g.*, Psychology, Experimental. Also called Inverted Subject Heading.

Inverted Pages. The arrangement of a book containing two separate works issued together, with or without an inclusive title page or cover title, and bound in such a way that one is inverted with respect to the other, having a title page at each end of the volume and end pages in the center. [Ca.]

Inverted Subject Heading. *See* Inverted Heading.

Issue (Circulation) (*n.*) 1. The number of books loaned during a given period. Synonymous with Circulation. 2. The book cards representing books loaned for a given period. (*v.*) To charge a book.

Issue (Edition, etc.). Specifically, a distinct group of copies of an edition, distinguished from the rest by more or less slight but well-defined variations in the printed matter.

Different issues* are those in which

*A *binding variant* does not necessarily indicate a different issue, since there may be several different (simultaneous or successive) bindings of the sheets of a single issue.

intentional** changes have been made without resetting the type for the whole work. Such issues may be the result of (a) the distribution of the sheets of a single impression among two or more publishers, those copies issued by each being distinguished by different imprint or title page and possibly different preliminary matter; (b) the issue of the sheets of an existing impression with a new or changed title page, preface, notes, or in a different number of volumes, etc.; or (c) a new impression for which revisions have been incorporated in the original type or plates, *e.g.,* a "revised (or corrected) impression." [Ca.]

Issue (Old maps). The number of impressions (copies) made at a given time without any change being made in the plate.

Issue (Periodical). *See* Number (Publication) (1).

Issue (Publishing). Specifically, to produce, or cause to be produced, books or other printed matter for sale or for private distribution. [C.]

Issue Desk. *See* Circulation Desk.

Issuing Department. *See* Circulation Department.

Issuing Office. The department, bureau, office, division, or other specific governmental body responsible for the issuing of a government publication.

Italic. A variety of type with letters that slope to the right, based originally on the handwriting of Italian official documents.

Jacket. *See* Book Jacket.

Jacket Cover. *See* Book Jacket.

Japanese or Japan Paper. 1. A soft thin paper made in Japan from the bark of the mulberry tree; used for proofs of engravings, etc. 2. An imitation of the Japanese-made paper.

Japanese Style. *See* Chinese Style.

Japanese Tissue. A very thin, strong, transparent tissue paper, often pasted on each side of old or worn paper to preserve it.

Joined Hand. A type of vertical handwriting with connected letters.

Joint. 1. Either of the two portions of the covering material that bend at the groove and along the flange when the covers of a bound book are opened. Sometimes called Inside Strip or Hinge. 2. (*pl.*) The reinforcements applied to the end linings, or to the combination of end papers and end signatures, designed to strengthen the binding.

Joint Author. A person who collaborates with one or more associates to produce a work in which the contribution of each is not separable from that of the others. [C.]

**Since in early printed books the composition and presswork were done by hand, it was possible for corrections, changes, and errors to be made during the course of printing. Resultant sheets, both corrected and uncorrected, were assembled in various accidental combinations, possibly issued at different times. To describe a copy which one has been unable to identify as belonging to an issue ' (the same differences common to a group of copies) the terms "*variant,*" "*variant copy,*" and "*state*" have all been used. Since best usage is still undecided there is no recommendation of a preferred term. "State" has been used also to describe condition.

Journal. 1. A periodical or a newspaper. 2. Specifically, a periodical issued by an institution, corporation, or learned society, containing current news and reports of activities and work in a particular field. 3. The record of proceedings or transactions of a learned society, or the daily record of a public body such as a legislature. 4. A person's daily record of his activities.

Junior. A personnel rating term added to titles of positions to indicate relative rank; applied usually to assistants who under supervision do the simpler kinds of nonsupervisory work or, in some cases more difficult work requiring special qualifications.

Junior Department. *See* Children's Department; Young People's Department.

Junior Undergraduate Library School. A school for education in librarianship that met minimum standards of the Board of Education for Librarianship of the American Library Association from 1925 to 1933 by being connected or affiliated with an approved library, college, or university, requiring for entrance one year of college work and meeting other requirements with respect to faculty, curriculum, and other factors. *Cf.* Type III Library School.

Justification. A printing 'operation that equalizes the lengths of type lines and adjusts cuts in the proper position in a form by the insertion of spaces.

Juvenile Department. *See* Children's Department.

Juveniles. Children's books.

Juvenilia. Works produced in youth, especially early works of distinguished authors.

Keepsake. *See* Giftbook.

Kern. The part of a type face that extends beyond the body.

Kettle Stitch. A stitch used in book sewing by means of which each signature is firmly united to the preceding one at head and tail. Also called Chain Stitch.

Key Word. *See* Catchword (2).

Keystoning. The effect produced in a projected image when the screen on which the image is projected is not perpendicular to the axis of projection. [M.]

Kip Calf. Leather made from the skins of neat cattle of intermediate size, *i.e.*, leather between calfskin and cowhide.

Kleidograph. A machine similar to a typewriter for writing New York point, a type for the blind no longer used.

L Sheet. A sheet of paper of letter size, usually 8x11 inches.

Label (Binding). A piece of paper or other material, printed or stamped, affixed to a book cover. The usual position is on the spine or the front cover.

Label Holder. A small frame, generally of metal, to hold a label. If it is on the end of a bookcase, it is also known as a Card Frame.

Label Title. The title of a fifteenth-century book printed in sentence form near the top of a separate leaf at the beginning of the book, and occasionally on the back of the last leaf, in place of, or in addition to, such a title at the front of the book.

Laboratory Collection. 1. A small group of books belonging to a college or a university library, kept in a laboratory, a professor's office, or a department office as a direct help in teaching a certain subject. 2. A group of books in a teacher-preparing institution, a library school, or other similar institution, organized for purposes of demonstration, practice, and project work.

Laboratory Work. In a library school, supervised practice closely related to a particular class assignment and usually directed by the instructor of the course.

Lacuna. A gap. (*pl.* lacunae.) Gaps in the collections of a library that need to be filled.

Laid Lines. The close thin lines in laid paper that show lighter than the rest of the paper; produced in the process of manufacture.

Laid Paper. Paper that shows close thin parallel lines crossed by heavier lines about an inch apart, which are produced in the process of manufacture.

Lamination. A method of repairing and protecting manuscripts and other material by the use of cellulose acetate foil fused with the paper by heat and pressure, or by the use of liquid sprays.

Lamp House. A small metal compartment in which the lamp of a projector is mounted. [M.]

Language Subdivision. 1. A subdivision according to language, as in catalog entries for sacred books, *e.g.*, Bible. English. 2. A subdivision by topic under a language division of a classification scheme, *e.g.*, Etymology, or Grammar, under English language.

Large Paper Copy or Edition. A copy or an edition of a book printed on paper of extra size, allowing wide margins, with letterpress the same as in the regular edition.

Latent Image. An invisible image produced by the action of light on the photosensitive material in a film. This latent image is made visible by development. [M.]

Law Binding. A style of plain full-leather binding (usually sheep), in light color, with two dark labels on back; now reproduced in buckram.

Law Buckram. A buckram book cloth made to resemble sheepskin in color.

Law Calf. 1. Uncolored calf. Practically obsolete. 2. A cream-colored, bark-tanned, smooth-surfaced calf, much used on the better grade of law bindings. 3. A misnomer for law sheep.

Law Sheep. Sheepskin in its natural

color; used largely for the binding of law books.

Layout. A plan prepared for a printer, or by a printer, showing general arrangement of matter, and of type, illustrations, etc., with indication of type styles and sizes.

Leader. A piece of blank film attached to the beginning of a roll of microfilm for threading into the projector and for the protection of the first frames of the roll. [M.]

Leaders. A line of dots, hyphens, or other characters, used to guide the eye across a space, as in indexes, tables, etc.

Leading. The spacing between lines of print, secured usually by inserting between the lines of type thin metal strips less than type high called "leads."

Leaf. 1. One of the units into which the original sheet or half sheet of paper, parchment, etc., is folded or divided to form a book. A leaf consists of two pages, one on each side, either or both of which may be blank, or may bear printing, writing, or illustration. [C.] 2. Gold leaf. 3. Thin metallic sheets, other than gold, used in lettering.

Leaflet. 1. In a limited sense, a publication of from two to four pages printed on a small sheet folded once, but not stitched or bound, the pages following in the same sequence as in a book. 2. In a broader sense, a small thin pamphlet.

Leather-bound. Either fully or partly bound in leather, but always with a leather back.

Ledger Charging System. An obsolete system for charging books in which the record was kept in an account book.

Legal Cap File. *See* Legal Size Vertical File.

Legal Size Vertical File. A File with drawers large enough to accommodate legal size paper. Also called Legal Cap File.

Legend. 1. A title or other descriptive text printed below an illustration or an engraving. 2. On a map, an explanation of symbols, etc., to aid in reading the map. 3. A story based on tradition rather than fact, but considered historical in the popular mind.

Legislative Manual. *See* State Manual.

Legislative Reference Service. Assistance given by a library in problems of government and legislation, especially in connection with proposed or pending legislation, sometimes including the drafting of bills.

Lending Department. *See* Circulation Department.

Lending Desk. *See* Circulation Desk.

Lens Aperture. The area of a lens, which can usually be adjusted by a mechanical diaphragm. [M.]

Let-in Note. *See* Cut-in Note.

Letter-by-letter Alphabetizing or Alphabeting. Arranging alphabetically, strictly according to letters, regardless of their division into words.

Letter Symbols (Size notation). *See* Size Letters.

Lettered Proof. A proof of an engraving with its title and names of artist, engraver, and printer engraved in the margin.

Lettering. 1. In binding, the process of marking a cover with title or other distinguishing characters, and, in a loose sense, with the accompanying ornamentation. 2. The result of this process.

Letterpress. (*a.*) Printed from raised surfaces, such as type, rather than by intaglio or lithographic processes. (*n.*) 1. Printed matter produced from raised surfaces, such as type. 2. Reading matter in a book as distinguished from the illustrations.

Levant. A high-grade morocco having a grain somewhat coarser than Turkey morocco; made from the skin of the Angora goat.

Level (Stack). *See* Deck.

Librarian. 1. A person responsible for the administration of a library. 2. The chief administrative officer of a library. 3. A professional member of a library staff. 4. Combined with name of department, type of work, kind of library, or with a personnel rating term, the term is used to designate the title of a staff member; *e.g.,* order librarian, children's librarian, branch librarian, senior librarian.

Librarian's Note. A critical annotation of a book, written to aid the librarian in the choice of books for the library and in recommending books to readers.

Librarianship. The application of knowledge of books and certain principles, theories, and techniques to the establishment, preservation, organization, and use of collections of books and other materials in libraries, and to the extension of library service.

Library. 1. A collection of books and similar material organized and administered for reading, consultation, and study. 2. A room, a group of rooms, or a building, in which a collection of books and similar material is organized and administered for reading, consultation, and study. 3. Synonymous with series as part of the collective title for a group of books issued in the same form by a publisher.

Library Administration. The active management of a library, including the formation and carrying out of policies and plans.

Library Agency. Any organized medium for the collection, distribution, and use of books through library activity; as, a library, a library commission, a branch library.

Library Binding. 1. A special form of bookbinding that has strength and durability to withstand severe library use. Distinguished from Edition Binding. 2. The processes employed in producing such a binding.

Library Board. *See* Board of Trustees.

Library Card. *See* Borrower's Card.

Library Center. A branch library in a regional library system.

Library Club. 1. In a school library, a club which assists in the work of the library and may or may not follow a reading program. 2. A local, district, or state group of librarians organized to meet for discussion and action on professional matters.

Library Commission. 1. An organization created by a state to promote library service within the state by the establishment, organization, and supervision of public and, sometimes, school libraries, and by the lending of books and other material to libraries and to communities without libraries. The term State Library Agency is replacing this term. 2. Occasionally, a local library board.

Library Corner. A book corner in which the covering material is not cut, the excess being taken up in two diagonal folds, one under each turn-in. Also called Dutch Corner, and sometimes, loosely, Round Corner. *Cf.* Mitered Corner and Square Corner.

Library Discount. Reduction from list price allowed to libraries by publishers, jobbers, local dealers, and other agents.

Library District. 1. An area in which the citizens have voted to assume a tax to support a public or a school library, according to legal provisions. 2. One of the sections into which a state is divided for the holding of library institutes. 3. One of the regional sections into which a state is divided to facilitate the establishment and maintenance of public libraries in accordance with a state plan.

Library Economy. The practical application of library science to the founding, organizing, and administration of libraries.

Library Edition. 1. A publisher's term for a series or a set of books, often all the works of an author, issued in a uniform style. The term is little used at present. 2. An edition prepared with an especially strong binding for library use. Also known as Special Library Edition and Special Edition.

Library Extension. The promotion of libraries and wider library service, by state, local, or regional agencies.

Library Hand or Handwriting. A standard type of vertical writing much used in the past for library records.

"Library Has" Statement. A note in a catalog entry for a serial indicating the library's holdings.

Library Hour. A regularly scheduled period which a student or a class spends in the library. Also called Library Period.

Library Inspector. *See* Library Organizer.

Library Instruction. Teaching readers how to use the library and its materials.

Library of Congress Card. One of the printed catalog cards issued by the Library of Congress.

Library of Congress Classification. A system of classification for books developed by the Library of Congress for its collections. It has a notation of letters and figures that allows for expansion.

Library of Congress Depository Catalog. A catalog containing a complete set of cards printed by the Library of Congress, placed without charge in certain libraries. Also called Depository Catalog.

Library Organizer. A member of a state library agency, such as a library commission, who inspects libraries, assists in establishing, organizing, and reorganizing libraries, and advises librarians in the state. Also called Library Visitor, Field Visitor, and, less frequently, Library Inspector and Inspector of Libraries.

Library Pass. *See* Admission Record.

Library Period. *See* Library Hour.

Library Permit. *See* Admission Record.

Library Planning. 1. Developing a plan for the design and construction of a library building or the buildings of a library system. 2. The formulation of comprehensive integrated plans for library objectives in city, county, region, state, or nation.

Library School. An agency which gives in a single academic year at least one co-ordinated professional curriculum in library science, for which credit for a full year of study is granted in accordance with the practice of the institution.

Library Science. The knowledge and skill by which printed or written records are recognized, collected, organized, and utilized.

Library Stamp (Binding). *See* Imprint (Binding) (1).

Library Trustees. *See* Board of Trustees.

Library Unit. A group of books sent to a classroom from a central school reservoir collection.

Library Visitor. *See* Library Organizer.

Libretto. The literary text of an extended vocal composition, such as an opera, oratorio, or cantata; a text intended for musical composition in one of these forms. [Ca.]

License. *See* Cum Licentia; Cum Privilegio.

Lichtdruck. *See* Collotype (1).

Lift, Book. *See* Book Lift; Book Conveyor.

Ligature. Two letters or characters connected by one or more strokes in common, as in ancient manuscripts; or two or more letters joined and cast on one type body, as ff. In printing, often called Double Letter.

Light Filter. *See* Filter. [M.]

Light-struck Film. Film that has been fogged by having light accidentally fall on it. [M.]

Lilliput Edition. *See* Miniature Book or Edition.

Limited Edition. An edition issued with a relatively small number of copies, to which consecutive numbers are generally assigned; sometimes issued, with superior paper and binding, in addition to a regular edition.

Limp Binding. A soft, flexible binding.

Limp Leather. A style of binding in full leather, without stiff boards.

Line Division Mark. A mark, usually a vertical line or double vertical lines, used in bibliographical transcription, primarily to indicate ends of lines. Also called Line-end Stroke, Dividing Stroke, and Upright Stroke.

Line Drawing. A drawing in lines.

Line-end Stroke. *See* Line Division Mark.

Line Ending. The right-hand ending of a line in a manuscript or a printed book.

Line Engraving. 1. An intaglio process of engraving in line on a copper or steel plate by means of a burin or graver. Also called, from material of plate, Copper Engraving, Copperplate Engraving, or Steel Engraving. 2. A print produced from such a plate.

Line Etching. *See* Zinc Etching.

Line Letter Type. An embossed line type for the blind based on roman type. Also known as Boston Line. *Obsolete.*

Linen. 1. A book cloth made of flax. 2. A book cloth made of cotton in imitation of genuine linen. 3. A book-cloth pattern that resembles the texture of linen.

Lining Paper. 1. The end paper which has one half pasted to the inner face of the cover and the other half free. When there is but one end paper at each end of the book the end papers coincide with the lining papers. When the fold of the end papers is lapped round the end gatherings and sewed with the book, the lining papers appear not to have conjugate leaves.

Lining papers may be blank, or they may bear text or illustration. They may be covered with silk or other fabric, or their place may be taken by a lining of other material or by doublures and their guard leaves. [C.] 2. A strong paper used for the end papers of books. 3. The paper used for lining the backs of heavy books, supplementing the lining fabric.

Linked Books. Separately bound books whose relationship with each other is indicated in various ways, such as collective title pages, mention in contents or other preliminary leaves, continuous paging, or continuous series of signature marks.

Linocut. *See* Linoleum Print.

Linoleum Print. A print made from a linoleum block by a relief process similar to that used for a wood-block print. Sometimes called Linocut.

List Price. The price quoted in a publisher's catalog.

Literature Search. Particularly in a special library, a systematic and exhaustive search for published material bearing on a specific problem or subject, with the preparation of abstracts for the use of the researcher; an intermediate stage between reference work and research, and to be differentiated from both.

Lithograph. A print produced by lithography.

Lithography. A planographic process of printing from a drawing made with a greasy chalk or ink on a special kind of porous stone, or some other substance, the printing ink, also greasy, adhering only to the lines drawn.

Lithophotography. *See* Photolithography.

Loan Department. *See* Circulation Department.

Loan Desk. *See* Circulation Desk.

Loan Record. *See* Circulation Record (1); Out Guide.

Loan System. *See* Charging System.

Local List. 1. A geographical list in Cutter's *Expansive Classification,* with numerical symbols to be used with any subject designation to indicate local division or relation. 2. A list prepared by W. P. Cutter, giving geographical and political divisions, accompanied by numbers, for use in dividing material geographically. 3. A list of books relating to a particular locality, as a town or county.

Local Subdivision. *See* Geographic Division.

Location Map. *See* Index Map.

Location Mark. A letter, word, group of words, or some distinguishing character added to catalog records, often in conjunction with the call number, to indicate that a book is shelved in a certain place, as in a special collection. Also called Location Symbol.

Location of Copies. Indication in a bibliography, union list, or union catalog, of libraries or collections where copies of the works listed may be found.

Location Symbol. 1. An identifying mark, such as a combination of letters, used in a bibliography, union list, or union catalog to indicate a library or a collection where a copy of a given work may be found. 2. A location mark (*q.v.*).

Loose Back. The back of a book in which the covering material is not glued to the back. Also called Hollow Back, Open Back, and Spring Back.

Lost Book. 1. A book known only by allusions to it or from quotations in the writings of contemporaneous authors. 2. A library book lost by a borrower, never returned by a borrower, or lost from shelves of the library.

Lost Book Indicator. In some libraries, a dummy put on a shelf in place of a lost book, marked with direction about disposition of the book if it is found.

Lower-case Letters. Small letters of a font, so called from their position in an old-style case for type.

Loxodrome. *See* Portolan Chart.

Machine-finished Paper. Paper made smooth but not very glossy by the pressure of calender rolls.

Maclure Library. One of the collections of books provided through a fund bequeathed by William Maclure and distributed about 1855 to clubs and societies of laborers that had established libraries.

Magazine. 1. A periodical for general reading, containing articles on various subjects by different authors, and generally fiction and poetry. 2. Originally, a monthly summary of news with a selection of miscellaneous items from daily and weekly publications.

Magazine Rack. *See* Rack.

Main Card. A catalog card bearing the main entry for a work.

Main Catalog. *See* Central Catalog (1).

Main Entry. A full catalog entry, usually the author entry, giving all the information necessary to the complete identification of a work. In a card catalog this entry bears also the tracing of all the other headings under which the work in question is entered in the catalog. The main entry, used as a master card, may bear in addition the tracing of related references and a record of other pertinent official data concerning the work. |Ca.|

Main Library. *See* Central Library.

Main Shelf List. *See* Central Shelf List (1).

Maintenance Department. *See* Building Department.

Majuscule. A capital or an uncial letter used in Greek and Latin manuscripts, as distinguished from a minuscule.

Make-up. In printing, the process of putting together the component parts of a predetermined unit, such as the assembling of text, illustrations, running heads, footnotes, etc., into pages.

Manière Criblée. *See* Dotted Print.

Manila Rope. A durable brown or buff paper made from manila hemp fibers. Also called Red Rope.

Manual. 1. A compact book that treats concisely the essentials of a subject; a handbook. 2. A book of rules for guidance.

Manual, Staff. *See* Staff Manual.

Manual, State. *See* State Manual.

Manufacturer's Catalog. *See* Trade Catalog (1).

Manuscript. 1. A work written by hand. 2. The handwritten or typewritten copy of an author's work before it is printed.

Manuscript Book. A handwritten book, as distinguished from a handwritten document, letter, or paper; particularly, one before, or at the time of, the introduction of printing.

Manuscript Map. An original or a compiled map, drawn but not printed. Loosely, any map drawn by hand.

Map. A representation of a part or the whole of the surface of the earth or of a celestial body, delineated on a plane surface, each point in the drawing intended to correspond to a geographical or a celestial position.

Maps may be of cities, villages, or smaller areas such as wards, districts, parks, campuses, etc., regardless of scale or extent of area. In cataloging, fictional maps are considered maps, but projected or hypothetical plans of an area are called plans. Aerial photographs and mosaic "maps" are designated as plates or illustrations. For star maps *see* Chart.

A map may be pictorial, or it may be used as background for exhibiting various facts, statistical, archaeological, historical, military and naval (except tactical), scientific, cultural, sociological, etc. For meteorological and hydrographic maps *see* Chart. [Ca.]

Map Rack. *See* Rack.

Marbled Calf. Calfskin treated so as to produce a marble-like effect. *Cf.* Mottled Calf.

Marbled Paper. Paper decorated with a design resembling marble by being dipped into a liquid on whose surface floating dyes have been worked into a pattern.

Margin. The space on a page outside the printed or written matter. The four margins are commonly designated as: head, or top; fore edge, outer, or outside; tail, or bottom; back, inner, inside, or gutter.

Marginal Note. A written or printed note in the margin of a page. Also called Sidenote and, sometimes, in the plural, Marginalia.

Marginalia. *See* Marginal Note.

Marker. *See* Bookmark; Register (4).

Market Letter. A name usually given to a bulletin of an investment house issued at regular intervals.

Marking. 1. The placing of call numbers on books and other library material. 2. In serials work, the placing of a mark of ownership, with note about disposition, on each piece checked.

Marks of Omission. Three dots in a group (...) used in catalogs and bibliographies to show omissions from matter transcribed. Commonly known as "Three Dots."

Master Film. *See* Master Negative Film. [M.]

Master Negative Film. An original negative, or a duplicate negative, not for use in a projector but reserved for the special purpose of making positive film copies for sale or distribution. Also called Master Film. [M.]

Matrix. 1. A mold of papier-mâché or other material from which a stereotype is cast. Frequently abbreviated to "mat." 2. A mold from which an electrotype is cast. 3. A mold from which type is cast in a type-setting machine. 4. A die used in a type-founding mold to form the type face.

Mechanical Binding. A generic term for metal or plastic flat-opening bindings, e.g., spiral binding.

Mechanical Charging. See Charging Machine.

Mechanical Processes. Nontechnical work in the preparation of books for use, such as collating, pasting, and marking.

Mechanics' Library. A type of subscription library that flourished in the middle of the nineteenth century, maintained primarily for the use of young workingmen and apprentices. Also called Apprentices' Library.

Media File. In a special library, a file containing information for the buyers of advertising space on the circulation, rates, column and type size of magazines and newspapers.

Membership List. A list of members of an association, with addresses and frequently biographical data; frequently issued only to members.

Memoir. 1. A record of a person's knowledge of, or investigations in, a special limited field, particularly when presented to a learned society. 2. A record of observation and research issued by a learned society or an institution; sometimes, in the plural, synonymous with transactions. 3. A memorial biography. 4. (pl.) A book of reminiscences by the writer.

Mending. Minor restoration of a book, not involving the replacement of any material or the separation of book from cover. Not so complete a rehabilitation as repairing.

Mercantile Library. A type of subscription library that flourished in the middle of the nineteenth century, designed primarily for the use of young merchants' clerks.

Merrill Book Number. A book number from a scheme devised by W. S. Merrill for arranging material in alphabetical order by means of numbers, or in chronological order by means of date abbreviations.

Messenger Notice. 1. An overdue notice delivered by a person representing the library for a book not returned upon receipt of a request by mail. 2. A notice sent by mail that unless a book is returned a messenger will be sent for it.

Messenger Service. 1. The delivery and collection of books by a library employee. 2. The collection of overdue books by a library employee or a Western Union messenger.

Mezzotint. 1. A method of engraving on copper or steel that reproduces tones through roughening the surface of the plate with a toothed instrument called a rocker or cradle, scraping of the burr thus raised, and burnishing, to secure variations of light. 2. A print made by this process.

Microcopy. See Microphotograph and Microphotography. [M.]

Microfilm. (n.) A negative or a positive microphotograph on film. The term is usually applied to a sheet of film or to a long strip or roll of film,

16 mm. or 35 mm. wide, on which there is a series of microphotographs. (*v.*) To make microphotographs. [M]

Micropane. A microphotograph on glass. [M.]

Microphotograph. A photographic reproduction so much smaller than the object photographed that optical aid is necessary to read or view the image. The usual range of reduction of printed material is from eight diameters to twenty-five diameters. Also called Microcopy. [M.]

Microphotography. The technique of making microphotographs. [M.]

Microplate. A microphotograph on metal. [M.]

Microprint. A positive microphotograph photographically printed on paper. [M.]

Microscopic Edition. *See* Miniature Book or Edition.

Microslide. A microphotograph mounted for projection. [M.]

Microstat. A direct negative microphotograph on paper, made from a negative image by a copying camera fitted with a prism. [M.]

Millboard. *See* Binder's Board.

Mimeograph. An apparatus for duplicating typewritten or handwritten material by means of a stencil.

Miniature. A picture painted by hand in an illuminated manuscript; so called from the extensive use of red paint (*minium*).

Miniature Book or Edition. A book of tiny size, generally two inches or less in height. Also called "Lilliput Edition" and Microscopic Edition.

Miniature Score. A common name for a score for orchestra or other instrumental ensemble published in a small (12mo or 16mo) size.

Minification. 1. The reduction of the dimensions of an object. 2. The reduction ratio. [M.]

Mint. In the same condition as when it came from publisher or printer, *i.e.*, new and unhandled.

Minuscule. A small letter in medieval handwriting.

Mitered. Indicating a binding ornamentation of straight lines that meet but do not cross each other.

Mitered Corner. A book corner in which a triangular piece of the covering material is cut off at the corner so that the turn-ins meet without overlapping.

Mixed Notation. Letters and figures or other symbols, used in combination to represent the divisions of a classification scheme.

Modern Roman. *See* Roman Type (2).

Monograph. A systematic and complete treatise on a particular subject, usually detailed in treatment but not extensive in scope. It need not be bibliographically independent. [C.]

Monographic Series. A series of monographic works issued in uniform style under a collective title by an academy, an association, a learned society, or an institution. The monographs may or may not be bibliographically independent, but they are usually related in subject or interest.

Monthly. A periodical issued once a month, with the possible omission of certain designated months, usually during the summer.

Moon Type. An embossed line type for the blind based on a greatly modified form of the roman capital letters. More easily learned than braille, it is used today by adults who are unable to master braille. Devised in 1849 by Dr. William Moon, a blind clergyman of Brighton, England.

Morgue. Formerly, a library in a newspaper office. The term originally referred specifically to biographical material collected or to obituaries prepared in advance of the deaths of well-known persons.

Morocco. 1. Leather manufactured from the skins of goats. 2. Sometimes, leather made from sheepskin finished to look like goatskin leather.

Mosaic Binding. A full-leather binding having a pattern formed by inlaying with colored leathers.

Mosaic "Map." A composite picture made up of two or more overlapping aerial photographs which, being in perspective or conic projection, represent on a true scale only those portions of the earth which are vertically below the center of the camera. [Ca.]

Mottled Calf. Calf that has been mottled with color dabbed on with sponges or wads of cotton. *Cf.* Sprinkled Calf, Speckled Calf, and Marbled Calf.

Mottled Sheep. Sheep for bookbinding, treated with colors in an irregular pattern.

Mounted. Attached by paste or glue to some other surface, as a picture or a page.

Movable Location. *See* Relative Location.

Multiple Copies. *See* Added Copy.

Municipal Library. 1. A public library established, maintained, and supported through taxation by a city, town, township, village, or school district. 2. A municipal reference library (*q.v.*).

Municipal Reference Library. A library maintained by a city for the use of city officials.

Municipal Reference Service. Assistance given by a library in problems of city government, particularly in connection with proposed or pending ordinances, often including the drafting of ordinances.

Museum Library. A group of specialized book collections maintained by a museum in the fields covered by its exhibits.

Name Authority File. *See* Authority List or File.

Name Catalog. A catalog arranged alphabetically by names of persons and places, whether used as authors or subjects.

Name File. *See* Authority List or File.

Name List. *See* Authority List or File.

Name Reference. A reference to the form of name selected for use in the catalog from alternating forms.

Narrow. Width less than three fifths of height, as, *narrow* octavo.

National Bibliography. A list (or, collectively, lists) of works published in a country; or, in an extended sense, of works about a country, by natives of a country living in that country or elsewhere, or written in the language of a country.

National Biography. 1. The branch of biography that treats of the lives of notable persons living in or associated with a particular country. 2. Collective biography of notable persons living in or associated with a particular country.

National Library. A library maintained by a nation.

Near-print. *See* Processed.

Needlework Binding. *See* Embroidered Binding.

Negative Film. *See* Negative Photograph; Negative Stock. [M.]

Negative Photograph. A photographic image in which the lights and shades existing in the original object are reversed. [M.]

Negative Stock. Photographic film intended for use in a camera. [M.]

Negro Branch. A branch of a public library maintained for the use of the negro population of a community.

Net Price. The price charged for a book after discounts are deducted. The term is little used now.

New York Point. An obsolete type for the blind, a variation of braille, in which the character was two dots high with a variable base of from one to four dots, and in which was adopted for the first time the principle of making the most frequently used symbols the simplest.

Newark Charging System. A single-entry method of recording book loans, in which the book cards are filed to form a time record and the borrowers' cards are retained by the borrowers.

News Bulletin. A digest of current news concerning or affecting the work of a special library's clientele or organization, usually issued daily and distributed to selected or key individuals, such as executives of the organization.

News Release. *See* Press Release.

Newsbook. 1. A pamphlet of the sixteenth and seventeenth centuries relating current events. *Cf.* Relation and Coranto. 2. After 1640 in England, a journal usually issued weekly, consisting at first of one sheet in quarto, later of two sheets, variously entitled Diurnall, Mercurius, Intelligence.

Newsletter. 1. A sixteenth- and seventeenth-century manuscript report of the day, written for special subscribers and issued irregularly or weekly. 2. A similar seventeenth-century report for special subscribers, sometimes set in scriptorial type and imitating the appearance of the earlier manuscript letter.

Newspaper. 1. A publication issued at stated and frequent intervals, usually daily, weekly, or semiweekly, which reports events and discusses topics of current interest. 2. Newsprint (q.v.).

Newspaper File. See File (1); Stick.

Newspaper Rack. See Rack.

Newspaper Rod. See Stick.

Newspaper Stack. 1. A specially planned stack for the storage of bound volumes of newspapers or any large flat books. 2. A part of an ordinary stack arranged so that newspaper volumes lying flat extend from one side of a double-faced bookcase to the other.

Newspaper Stand. See Rack.

Newspaper Stick. See Stick.

Newsprint. Cheap paper made largely from wood pulp, on which newspapers are printed. Also called Newspaper.

Niger Morocco. A morocco made from native-tanned Sudanese goatskin, produced on the banks of the River Niger. Sometimes shortened to Niger.

Nihil Obstat. Literally, "Nothing hinders," a statement of sanction for publication given by a Catholic book censor, found usually on verso of title page or following leaf.

Ninety-one Rules. The catalog code prepared by Sir Anthony Panizzi and a committee, for use in compiling the catalog of the British Museum.

Nitrate Film. See Cellulose Nitrate. [M.]

Noncommercial Publication. As used in special libraries, a publication issued as a secondary nonprofit activity by such organizations as associations, foundations, business corporations, social agencies, universities, government bodies, museums, committees, etc. It is often processed rather than printed; and it may be distributed on a cost, subscription, or membership basis, or may be issued for limited distribution and therefore be available on a courtesy basis only.

Nonfiction. Books other than novels and stories for children.

Nonparliamentary Paper. A publication prepared by one of the various departments of the British government independently without direct Parliamentary command.

Nonperforate Film. Film without perforations or sprocket holes. [M.]

Nonprofessional Assistant. See Clerical Assistant; Subprofessional Assistant.

Nonresident's Card. A borrower's card issued to a patron who does not reside within the territory regularly served by the library, usually upon payment of a small fee. Sometimes known as Fee Card.

Notation. A system of symbols, generally letters and figures, used separately or in combination, to represent the divisions of a classification scheme.

Note. 1. A statement explaining the text of a book or adding material to it, printed on the same page as the text, or at end of book or chapter. 2. A concise statement after imprint and collation in a catalog or bibliography entry, giving added information, such as name of series, bibliographical information, or contents. In cataloging, the term is sometimes limited to an item on a catalog card below the collation and the main body of the card.

Number (Classification). *See* Class Number.

Number (Publication). 1. A single numbered or dated issue of a series, a periodical, or a serial publication; generally so slight in extent that two or more may be bound together to form a volume. 2. One of the numbered fascicles of a literary, artistic, or musical work issued in instalments, ordinarily in paper wrappers, and called "number" by the publisher.* [C.]

"Number Trade." *See* Number (Publication) (2).

---

* This method of distribution was called the "number trade"; the completed work is known as a "part-issue."

Numbered Column. A column of a page having a number at its head.

Numbered Copy. A copy of a book in a limited edition, to which a number has been assigned.

Numbered Entry. One of the entries designated by consecutive numbers in a bibliography or a printed book catalog.

Object Lens. *See* Objective. [M.]

Objective. The image-forming lens of a camera or projection. Also called Object Lens and Projection Lens. [M.]

Oblong. Width exceeding height, as, *oblong* octavo.

Octavo. 1. Format: a book printed on full-size sheets folded to make eight leaves or sixteen pages. 2. Size: according to the American Library Association scale, a book which measures 20 to 25 cm. in height.

Offcut. Specifically, that portion of a printed sheet which in certain formats, as duodecimo, is so imposed that it must be cut off and folded separately before insertion within the center fold of the quire. The inserted part is called the inset, and usually bears a signature mark to indicate its position in gathering; *e.g.*, the first leaf of a quire of six leaves might be lettered B, and its third leaf (the first leaf of the inset) would usually be marked B2. [C.]

Official Catalog. A catalog for the use of the library staff only.

Official Gazette. *See* Gazette (3).

Official Name. The legal name of a governmental agency or a corporate body.

Offprint. An impression of an article, chapter, or other portion of a larger work, printed from the type or plates of the original and separately issued, sometimes with one or more additional pages or leaves. Called also Separate. [C.]

Offset. 1. A mark or smut on a printed or white sheet caused by contact with a freshly printed sheet on which the ink is wet. Sometimes called Setoff. 2. A lithographic process of printing by which the image, rendered directly on metal or stone, or reproduced photographically on a metal plate, is first transferred to a rubber blanket and then to paper. Also called Offset Lithography, Offset Printing, Offset Process.

Offset Lithography. *See* Offset (2).

Offset Printing. *See* Offset (2).

Offset Process. *See* Offset (2).

Old Style. A general style of roman or italic type based on the roman and italic type faces of the fifteenth and early sixteenth centuries and characterized chiefly by angular design and slanting serifs.

Olin Book Number. An author number from a scheme devised by Charles R. Olin for arranging collective biography in a separate group from individual biography when class number is the same.

Omission, Marks of. *See* Marks of Omission.

Omnibus Book or Volume. A large one-volume collection of reprints of several novels or other works of an author originally published separately, or a similar volume of short stories, or of other types of literature, by several authors.

Omnibus Review. A critical article that discusses a group of books of a certain type or in a particular field.

One-card System. *See* Single-entry Charging System.

One-line. *See* Title-a-line.

One On. *See* All Along.

One Sheet On. *See* All Along.

Onion Skin. A thin, translucent, glazed paper resembling the outer skin of an onion.

Onlay. A decorative panel of paper or other material, glued to the front cover of a book without preliminary blanking of the cover to receive it. *Cf.* Inlay.

Ooze Leather. Leather made from calfskins by a special process, producing on the flesh side a soft, finely-granulated finish like velvet or suede. The term is incorrectly used with reference to sheepskin.

Opaque Screen. A diffuse reflecting surface, such as unglazed paper, on which a projected image is viewed. [M.]

Open Access. *See* Open Shelves.

Open-air Reading Room. Outdoor reading space provided for patrons who wish to use books at the library.

Open Back. *See* Loose Back.

Open-back Case. *See* Slipcase.

Open Entry. A catalog entry which provides for the addition of information concerning a work of which the library does not have a complete set, or about which complete information is lacking. [Ca.]

Open Joint. *See* French Joint.

Open-letter Proof. A proof of an engraving with an inscription engraved in outlined letters.

Open Reserve. A reserved book collection to which access is not restricted.

Open Score. The score of a musical work for two or more voices, in which each voice part is printed on a separate staff.

Open-shelf Collection. 1. Any collection of books in a library to which the public has unrestricted access. 2. A group of recent books and standard works of general appeal placed on easily accessible shelves, generally in a circulation department.

Open Shelves. Library shelves to which readers have direct access for the examination of books. Also called Open Stack.

Open Stack. *See* Open Shelves.

Opened. The folded edges of an uncut book divided by hand for reading. Not to be confused with "cut."

Opening. The two opposite pages of an open book.

Operations Department. *See* Building Department.

Optical Flats. *See* Flats. [M.]

Optical System. A combination of lenses, mirrors, or prisms. [M.]

Opus Number. A number assigned to a work, or a group of works, of a composer, generally indicating order of composition or of publication.

Order Card. A form for recording information used in ordering a book.

Order Department or Division. The administrative unit that has charge of selecting and acquiring books and other material by purchase and of keeping the necessary records of these additions; and in many libraries, of securing books and other material by gift and exchange. Sometimes called, when its work is more inclusive, Acquisition Department.

Order Librarian. 1. A librarian in charge of the work of an order department. For a department of two or more, the terms Chief of Order Department and Chief Order Librarian are coming into use and are to be preferred. *Cf.* Chief. 2. A professional assistant in an order department, as a junior order librarian.

Organization File. In a special library, a collection of material about associations, institutions, and other nonprofit organizations; *e.g.,* annual reports, lists of officers and members, statements of purpose, lists of publications, and other data on specific organizations.

Organization (or Company) History File. In a special library, a file of material written or published by or about the organization of which the library is a part, as instructional bulletins, standard procedures, reports and surveys of its work, periodical and newspaper articles. Such a file is frequently designated by the name of the organization.

Original Binding. The binding that was originally applied to a particular copy of a book, without regard to priority of issue.

Original Edition. *See* First Edition.

Original Parts. A term describing the first edition of a work when issued in numbered parts with wrappers.

Original Sources. *See* Source Material.

Ornament. *See* Printer's Ornament.

Ornamental Initial. *See* Initial Letter.

Orthochromatic Film. A photographic film that is sensitive to yellow and green light as well as to blue and violet light. [M.]

Out Guide. In special libraries, a form card on which is recorded the charge for vertical file material. It is substituted for the borrowed publication and is large enough to be visible above the folder.

Out of Boards. An obsolete style of binding similar to "in boards," but with the boards projecting beyond the trimmed edges. Short for "cut out-of-boards."

Out of Print. Not obtainable through the regular market, since the publisher's stock is exhausted.

Out of Stock. Not available from the publisher until his stock is replenished.

Outer Indention. *See* "First" indention.

Outsert. An extra double leaf added to a printed signature around the outside, and forming a part of a given gathering.

Outside Source. As used by special librarians, a source of information outside their own organizations.

Outside User. In special libraries, a person outside its own clientele who may occasionally be permitted to use the library of a private organization.

Over-size or Over-sized Book. A book which, because of its larger format, cannot stand on the regular shelves of a library.

Overcasting. Hand sewing in which each section is sewn through and over the binding edge. In older usage, a generic term including oversewing and whipstitching.

Overdue Book. A book not returned on time by a borrower.

Overdue Notice. A postcard or letter sent to a borrower who has failed to return on time books or other library materials charged to him.

Oversewing. Sewing, by hand or machine, through the edge of each section in consecutive order, using preformed holes through which the needle passes.

Ownership Mark. A bookplate, stamp, label, or the like, identifying material as library property.

Oxford Corners. Border rules that cross and project beyond each other, as on title pages and book covers.

P Slip. A piece of paper approximately three by five inches; so called because it is the same size as the former small-sized United States postal cards.

Package Library. A collection of pamphlets and clippings on a particular topic, loaned by a library agency to an individual or a group.

Padding. *See* Filler.

Page. 1. One side of a leaf. 2. A part-time or a full-time assistant who carries books to and from the stack and does other routine work, chiefly in the stack and the circulation department. Also called Runner.

Page-head. *See* Headline (1).

Page Proof. A proof from matter made up into pages after corrections in the galley proof have been made.

Page Station. A desk, usually near the stack, where a page is stationed to get books when requested.

Pagination. 1. A system of numerals or other characters, or a combination of these, by which the pages of a book or manuscript are marked to indicate their order; an instance of this. *Cf.* Folio (3). 2. That part of the collation which states the number of pages, or pages and leaves, contained in a book. Also called Paging. [Ca.]

Pagination, Continuous. *See* Continuous Pagination.

Paging. *See* Pagination (2).

Paleography (Palaeography). The study of the early forms of handwriting, and the deciphering of ancient and medieval manuscripts. It is a basis for textual criticism.

Palimpsest. A manuscript written on a surface from which one or more earlier writings have been erased as completely as possible. Sometimes known as Rescript.

Palimscope. A small instrument about the size of a reading glass that forms a concentrated ultra-violet light source, designed for reading palimpsests and for use in other forms of research.

Palladium. A silver-colored precious metal of the platinum family, recently developed in a leaf form for lettering on book covers.

Pamphlet. 1. In a restricted technical sense, an independent publication consisting of a few leaves of printed matter stitched together but not bound; usually enclosed in paper covers. While independent in the sense that each pamphlet is complete in itself it is a common custom to issue pamphlets in series, usually numbered consecutively. In local library practice, there is variation in the maximum number of leaves or pages allowed under the term. For the purposes of statistics and method, some libraries set the limit at 80 pages (originally based on the equivalent of five printed sheets folded to octavo); others consider "about 100 pages" sufficient restriction. [Ca.]

From the bindery point of view, a pamphlet is any collection of leaves, paper-bound or self-covered, consisting of 64 pages or less.

2. A brief controversial treatise on a topic of current interest, usually religious or political; common in England from the sixteenth to the eighteenth century.

Pamphlet Binder. A cover of pasteboard, with a gummed stitched binding strip, for holding one or more pamphlets.

Pamphlet Binding. 1. Binding done by a printer or for a printer, in which the sheets, as they come from the press, are wire-stitched. The term applies both to pamphlets and to magazines. 2. The manner in which pamphlets and magazines are bound as they come from the publisher; usually wire-stitched, either side-stitched or saddle-stitched.

Pamphlet Box. An open or a closed box for holding a number of pamphlets. Sometimes called Pamphlet File.

Pamphlet File. *See* Pamphlet Box.

Pamphlet Laws. *See* Session Laws.

Pamphlet-style Library Binding. A style of binding for a pamphlet or a thin group of pamphlets when use is expected to be infrequent. Its characteristics are side stitching, usually with wire, and covers with cloth hinges, usually of plain boards, heavy paper, paper-covered boards, or thin lightweight cloth, cut flush, without gold lettering.

Pamphlet Volume. A volume composed of a number of separate pamphlets bound together either with or without a general title page or table of contents.

Panchromatic Film. A photographic film that is sensitive to the entire visible spectrum. [M.]

Panel. 1. A square or rectangular space on a cover, enclosed by lines, or sunk. 2. A space on the backstrip, between any two bands or between two parallel lines or sets of lines.

Paper. 1. A substance made in the form of thin sheets or leaves from rags, straw, bark, wood, or other fibrous material, for various uses. 2. A printed or written document or instrument; a writing, as a bill, note, or essay; as, a *paper* read before a society. 3. A printed sheet appearing periodically; a newspaper; a journal; as, a daily *paper.* [By permission; from Webster's *New International Dictionary,* Second Edition, copyright, 1934, 1939, by G. & C. Merriam Co.]

Paper-backed. *See* Paper-bound.

Paper Boards. *See* Boards.

Paper-bound. Bound simply with a paper cover. Also called Paper-backed.

Paperback. A cheap book in paper covers.

Papermark. *See* Watermark.

Papyrus. 1. A writing material of the ancient Egyptians, Greeks, and Romans, made of longitudinal strips of fiber from the papyrus plant, *Cyperus papyrus*, placed in layers at right angles. 2. A manuscript on this material.

Paragraph Indention. *See* "Second" Indention.

Parchment. Usually, the skin of a lamb, sheep, goat, or young calf, prepared by treatment with oil instead of tanning as a writing material and, formerly, as a binding material. *Cf.* Vellum, with which the term is now virtually interchangeable. (The distinction today among collectors of manuscripts is that *vellum* is a more refined form of skin, while *parchment* is a cruder form, usually thick, harsh, and less highly polished than vellum.)

Parentheses. *See* Curves.

Parish Library. 1. A library maintained by a parish, *i.e.*, a local division in Louisiana corresponding to a county. 2. One of the libraries sent from England to the American colonies for the clergy and their congregations through the efforts of Rev. Thomas Bray and his associates. Also called Bray Library.

Parliamentary Paper. A paper ordered to be printed by one or the other of the British Houses of Parliament or required for parliamentary business.

Parochial Library. *See* Parish Library.

Part. 1. One of the subordinate portions into which a volume has been divided by the publisher. It usually has a special title, half title, or cover title, and may have separate or continuous pagination, foliation, or register, but it is included under the collective title page or cover title of the volume which is intended to contain it. It is distinguished from a fascicle by being a unit rather than a temporary division of a unit. For Part as synonymous with Volume, *see* the definition of the latter. [C.] 2. The music for any one of the participating voices or instruments in a musical work. 3. The written or printed copy of such a part for the use of a singer or player.

Part Binding or Parti-binding. A style of binding in which the volume has a cloth back with paper sides, or, sometimes, a paper back with sides of different paper, but is without corners of the same material as the back.

Part Issue. An issue which has been distributed in instalments, usually in paper wrappers. [Ca.]

Part Signature. *See* Volume or Part Signature.

Partial Title. One which consists of a secondary part of the title as given on the title page. It may be a catch title, subtitle, or alternative title. [C.]

Pass, Library. *See* Admission Record.

Paste-down (or Board Paper). That half of the lining paper which is pasted to the inner face of the cover. [C.]

Paste-in. A revision of, or an addition to, a text, supplied after the original printing and pasted on or opposite the page to which it applies.

Pattern. In binding magazines and the like, a sample volume, sample back, rub-off, and/or other data used for matching the style.

Pay Duplicate Collection. *See* Rental Collection.

Pay Plan. *See* Classification and Pay Plan for Library Positions.

Pencil Dater. A metal device holding a rubber date stamp, that may be fastened to the end of a pencil.

Perforations. The small holes on one or both sides of a strip of film, used to drive the film through the camera, the processing machine, or the projecting machine. Also called Sprocket Holes. [M.]

Period Division. 1. A division of a classification scheme for works covering a limited period of time. 2. A subdivision of a subject heading which shows the period treated.

Period Printing. The production or reproduction of books not on the model of any particular edition, but in the style of the period when the book was first published or with which it is concerned.

Periodical. A publication witn a distinctive title intended to appear in successive (usually unbound) numbers or parts at stated or regular intervals and, as a rule, for an indefinite time. Each part generally contains articles by several contributors.

Newspapers, whose chief function it is to disseminate news, and the memoirs, proceedings, journals, etc., of societies are not considered periodicals under the rules for cataloging. [Ca.]

Periodical Department or Division. 1. The part of a library where current issues of periodicals and other serials are kept for reading. 2. The administrative unit in charge of handling periodicals, which may include ordering, checking, preparation for binding, etc. Also called Periodicals Department.

Periodical Index. 1. An index to a volume, several volumes, or a set of a periodical. 2. An index to a group of periodicals, generally issued periodically and usually cumulative.

Periodical Rack. *See* Rack.

Permit. *See* Admission Record; Stack Permit.

Persian Morocco. A so-called "morocco" made not from goatskin, but from the skin of a hairy sheep peculiar to India.

Personal Name Entry. The record of a book in a catalog under the name of an individual.

Phonogram. A character in writing that stands for a sound rather than an object or an idea.

Photo-litho Offset. *See* Photo-offset.

Photo-offset. Offset printing in which the image is reproduced on a metal plate by photography. Also called Photo-litho Offset, Photo-offset Printing, Photo-offset Process.

Photo-offset Printing or Process. *See* Photo-offset.

Photocopy. A direct photographic copy, such as a blueprint, usually made without a camera. [M.]

Photoduplication. Duplication by the use of photography. [M.]

Photoengraving. 1. The process of reproducing print, pictures, etc., by photographing the original on a metal plate and etching the plate with acid to give a relief printing surface. 2. A print made by this process.

Photoflood Bulb. An electric light with a filament normally designed for a much lower voltage than that on which the lamp is operated. It gives an intense light but is short-lived. [M.]

Photogelatine Process. *See* Collotype (1).

Photographic Facsimile. A reproduction of printing by a photographic method.

Photographic Film. *See* Film. [M.]

Photogravure. 1. A process of engraving that combines the photographic action of light on a chemically grained metal plate and etching. 2. A print produced by this method.

Photolithography. A lithographic process of reproducing print and pictures that involves photographing the original on a lithographic stone or some other surface, such as a thin metal plate. Also called Lithophotography.

Photomechanical Process. Any one of the processes of reproducing pictures, print, etc., that uses plates or blocks prepared by means of photography and mechanical or chemical action rather than by hand. Also called Process Engraving and Process Work.

Photomicrography. The process of obtaining enlarged photographic images of minute objects. [M.]

Photoprint. 1. A photographic copy made by contact printing. 2. A photographic copy made with a camera. [M.]

Photostat. 1. A specially constructed camera for reproducing books, maps, etc., which makes copies directly on sensitized paper without films or plates. 2. A trade name for such a camera. 3. A copy made by this device. Also called Photostatic Copy or Photostatic Print.

Photostatic Copy or Print. *See* Photostat.

Phototype. *See* Collotype (1).

Piano-vocal Score. A common form of publication for musical works originally composed for chorus and/or solo voices and orchestra. Examples are: cantatas, oratorios, and operas. Often called also "vocal score," a piano-vocal score of such a work consists of the original vocal parts and an arrangement for piano of the orchestral accompaniment.

Pica. Originally, a type size about 1/6 inch high. Now, the basic unit of the point system of measurement, being equal to 12 points or about 1/6 inch.

Pictograph. 1. In ancient forms of writing, a picture used to represent an idea. 2. A writing composed of pictographs.

Pictorial Map. A map containing pictures that indicate distribution of physical and biological features, social and economic characteristics, etc.

Picture Book. A book consisting wholly or chiefly of pictures, adapted to the interests and needs of younger children.

Picture or Art File. A collection of pictures, photographs, illustrations, prints, and clippings.

Picture Story Book. A book consisting of illustrations accompanied by explanatory text, narrative in form, and adapted to the interests and reading ability of younger children.

Piece. One of a variety of items of differing character (*e.g.*, pamphlets, broadsides, plates, facsimiles, sheet music) published or assembled as a collection. [Ca.]

Pigeonhole. *See* Bin.

Pigskin. Leather made from the skin of a pig.

Pinhead Morocco. A morocco of the hard-grained type, but with the grain smaller and less distinct than in the morocco called "hard-grained."

Pirated Edition. An edition published illegally, *e.g.*, an edition issued in violation of copyright privilege. Also called Pirated Reprint.

Place Division. *See* Geographic Division.

Place of Printing. The city or town in which a book is printed.

Place of Publication. The city or town where the publishing house that issues a book is located.

Placement. The orientation of the text within the frame.
Placement 1. The lines of text across the entire width of the film.
Placement 2. The lines of text parallel to the edge of the film.
Placement 3. The lines of text halfway across the width of the film, another page occupying the other half of the film.
Placement 4. The lines of text only one quarter across the width of the film. [M.]

Plain Title Edition. *See* Departmental Edition.

Plan. 1. A delineation in a horizontal, vertical, or oblique plane, showing the relative position of the parts of an architectural (including naval), or engineering structure. For working drawings of an individual part of such a structure, or for schemes for electrical or mechanical equipment, *see* Diagram. [Ca.] 2. A drawing, in a horizontal plane, showing the arrangement of (a) features in a landscape design, *e.g.*, a garden, a park, an estate; (b) position of streets and buildings in a projected town, zoned area, or similar development; (c) furniture and furnishings in a building or room, *e.g.*, an interior, a stage setting and properties, seats in an auditorium. Planting plans for a flower border are to be considered diagrams. For plans showing (a) the arrangement of equipment for games or athletics, or for efficiency in business, manufacturing, etc.; (b) the relative location of musical instruments in an orchestra; or (c) the details of an individual piece of furniture or equipment, *see* Diagram. [C.] 3. A graphic presentation of a tactical military or naval plan. [C.]

Planographic Printing. Printing from a flat surface, as in lithography and offset printing, in distinction from relief printing and intaglio printing.

Plant Publication. *See* House Organ.

Plastic Binding. A type of flat-opening binding used for pamphlets, commercial catalogs, etc. The single leaves and the separate front and back covers are fastened by means of a specially cut piece of synthetic plastic having prongs (combs) that pass through slots near the binding edge and are curled back within the cylinder thus formed by the plastic.

Plate.* *A* full page of illustration on a leaf which normally is blank on the other side. The reverse may, however, bear a descriptive legend, the title of the work, or another plate. The leaf is usually of special (heavy) paper and may or may not be included in the pagination. [Ca.]

Plate (Printing). 1. A piece of metal, usually of copper, nickel, or zinc, that bears matter to be printed, whether printing be relief, intaglio, or planographic. 2. An electrotype or a stereotype.

Plate Mark or Line. The line made by the edge of the plate in an intaglio engraving, which is slightly depressed from the surrounding paper in the process of printing.

Plate Number. A serial number assigned by a music publisher to each publication for purposes of record and identification. It appears usually at the bottom of each page and sometimes on the title page, and may be used as a clue to date of publication. Also called Publication Number.

Plate Revision. A revision confined to changes in parts of the printing plates, without entire resetting of the type.

Plating. The process of pasting bookplates in books.

Pneumatic Book Carrier. A system of tubes through which cartridges containing books are propelled by air pressure or by vacuum.

---

* This term originates from the engraved sheet of metal from which an impression of the illustration might be taken.

Pneumatic Tubes. A system of tubes through which cartridges containing call slips, etc., are propelled by air pressure or by vacuum.

Pocket. *See* Book Pocket; Borrower's Pocket; Cover Pocket.

Point. 1. A unit of measurement of type characters in their relation to each other. In America it is based on the pica body divided into twelve equal parts or points, each point being .01384 inch, or very nearly 1/72 inch. 2. A book collector's term for a particular characteristic of text, type, form, etc., that distinguishes one issue of an edition from another.

Pointillé. A kind of binding decoration consisting of dots or points.

Polyglot. Containing the text in several languages, *e.g.,* a polyglot Bible.

Polygraphy. Works consisting of several works, or extracts from several works, by one or many authors.

Popular Copyright. An inexpensive reprint issued by the original publisher or by a publisher of cheap editions through arrangement with the original publisher.

Popular Library. 1. A public library. *Obsolete.* 2. In a departmentalized library, a collection of books of general interest.

Popular Name. A shortened, abbreviated, or simplified form of the official name of a governmental agency or other corporate body, by which it is commonly known.

Portfolio. A case for holding loose papers, engravings, or similar material, consisting of two covers joined together at the back and usually tied at the front and the ends.

Portolan Chart. An early type of map for guiding mariners in coastwise sailing; usually in manuscript. Also called Loxodrome and Compass Map.

Portolano (Portolan, Portulan). A medieval book for mariners, consisting of sailing directions, with descriptions of harbors and seacoasts, and illustrated with charts.

Portrait. A likeness of a person, especially of the face, presumably made from life, by painting, drawing, engraving, photography, sculpture (including bas-relief), silhouette, etc. A picture of such a likeness. If it is unnamed, it is considered a portrait if the person may easily be identified in the book. In collation, the term is generally not used for the following: an actor in character; a caricature or an effigy; a person secondary in importance to the scene or event; types in ethnology, etc. (even though named); a mosaic; a death mask; portraits incidental to a decorative design; coins, postage stamps, etc. [Ca.]

Positive Film. *See* Positive Photograph; Positive Stock. [M.]

Positive Photograph. A photographic image in which the lights and shades are in the same order as in the object. [M.]

Positive Stock. Photographic film designed for making motion picture positive prints but frequently used in microphotographing cameras to obtain the original negative. [M.]

Possible Purchase File. *See* Want List (1).

Posthumous Work. A work first published after the author's death.

Postprofessional Education. Education for professional improvement undertaken by an individual librarian on his own initiative, without expense to the library, by such means as travel, further study in librarianship or in subject fields, library conferences and institutes, etc.

Powdered. *See* Semé.

Practice Work. *See* Field Work.

Prebound. *See* Pre-library-bound.

Preface. A note preceding the text of a book, which states the origin, purpose, and scope of the work and sometimes contains acknowledgments of assistance. To be distinguished from introduction, which deals more with the subject of the book.

Preface Date. The date given at the beginning or end of the preface. [C.]

Pre-library-bound. Of new books, bound in library binding prior to or at the time of original sale. Called Prebound for short.

Preliminaries. *See* Preliminary matter.

Preliminary Edition. An edition issued in advance of a permanent edi-

tion, sometimes for criticism before the final edition is published.

Preliminary Leaf. One of the unnumbered leaves, printed on one or both sides, preceding the numbered pages or leaves at the beginning of a book. [C.]

Preliminary Matter. The printed portion which precedes the text of a work. It includes some or all of the following: half title, frontispiece, general and special title pages, dedication, preface or foreword, table of contents, list of illustrations, introduction. This material is usually printed last of all, and as a separate signature or signatures with individual numeration. Called also Front Matter, and Preliminaries. [C.]

Preparation or Preparations Division. The administrative unit in charge of cataloging, classification, and the physical preparation of books for the shelves, and in some libraries, of other routines, such as order work, accessioning, and inventory. The term Processing Department is sometimes used.

Preprint. An impression printed in advance of regular publication, as of a periodical article, or part of a book.

Presentation Copy. A copy of a book bearing an inscription of presentation, generally by the author; or a copy of a book presented by the publisher.

Press. In England, a free-standing double-faced bookcase. In American libraries: formerly, a bookcase; at present, a single-faced series of tiers placed end to end.

Press Release. An official or authoritative statement giving information for publication in newspapers or periodicals on a specified date; usually in mimeographed form. Also known as Release and News Release.

Pressmark. A symbol indicating the room, case, and sometimes shelf, where a book is kept.

Pressure Plate. A heavy glass plate laid on material being microfilmed to keep it flat. See also Flats. [M.]

Primary Sources. See Source Material.

Princeps Edition or Princeps. See First Edition.

Print. Any picture reproduced by any printing process. The term is generally applied to what are often called "fine prints," e.g., etchings, line engravings, mezzotints, etc., especially those etched or engraved by the artist who made the design.

Printed As Manuscript. 1. Printed from manuscript which has not had final editorial revision. 2. Printed for private circulation, i.e., not to be quoted or sold. [C.]

Printed But Not Published. Printed, but not offered for sale by the publisher.

Printer. The person, or firm, by whom a book is printed, as distinguished from the publisher and the bookseller by whom it is issued and sold. [C.]

Printer, Continuous. See Continuous Printer. [M.]

Printer, Step. See Step Printer. [M.]

Printer's Device. See Printer's or Publisher's Mark.

Printer's Flower. See Floret (1).

Printers' Gothic. See Sans-serif.

Printer's or Publisher's Mark. An emblem or design used by a printer or a publisher to identify his work. Devices now in use are usually those of publishers rather than printers. Also known as Printer's Device or Publisher's Device, and Device.

Printer's Ornament. A type design with which a printed page is decorated, as a border, a headpiece, a tailpiece. Also known as Ornament.

Printer's Slip. Catalog card copy prepared on a slip for printing.

Printing (Edition, etc.). See Impression (Edition, etc.).

Printing (Microphotography). The process of making a copy from a photographic image by photographic contact printing or projection, usually producing a positive from a negative.

Printing Hand. See Disjoined Hand.

Private Library. A library not supported by taxation, especially a library belonging to an individual.

Private Press. One which produces books for a limited clientele; the editions are small and but rarely distributed through trade channels. Usually the books are finely printed, frequently by hand press. [C.]

Privately Illustrated. *See* Extra Illustrated.

Privately Printed. Issued for private distribution only, or issued from a private press and not offered for sale through the trade. [C.]

Privilege. *See* Cum Licentia; Cum Privilegio.

Procedure Manual. A compilation of procedures for performing specific tasks or for fulfilling the duties of a particular position in a special library. It is usually more detailed than, but otherwise comparable with, the staff manual of a general library except for the elimination of personnel matters, which are usually contained, in the case of corporations, in the employee handbook.

Proceedings. The published record of a meeting of a society or other organization, frequently accompanied by abstracts or reports of papers presented. *Cf.* Transactions.

Process Color Printing. A photomechanical process of reproducing pictures in color by the use of separate half-tone plates for two or more colors, prepared by means of color filters. Often called, from number of plates used, Three-color Process, Four-color Process.

Process Engraving. *See* Photomechanical Process.

Process Slip. A card or slip, sometimes a printed form, which accompanies a book through the catalog department, acquiring on its way all the information and directions necessary for cataloging fully. Also called Catalog Card Copy, Catalog Slip, Cataloger's Slip, Cataloging Process Slip, Copy Slip, Guide Slip, Routine Slip, Work Slip.

Process Work. *See* Photomechanical Process.

Processed. Reproduced by duplicating processes other than ordinary printing, as by mimeograph, multigraph, rotoprint, multilith, etc. Also called Near-print. Applied especially to government publications.

Processing. The operation of developing, fixing, washing, drying, and inspecting film. [M.]

Processing Department. *See* Preparation or Preparations Division.

Proctor Order. The system of arranging incunabula developed by Robert Proctor. The arrangement is chronological, based on the earliest date of printing, under the following groupings: by country, by place under the country, and by printer under the place.

Professional Assistant. A member of the professional staff performing work of a professional grade which requires training and skill in the theoretical or scientific parts of library work as distinct from its merely mechanical parts. The term is applied to all the professional staff except the chief librarian, associate or assistant chief librarians, and heads of departments and other administrative divisions of a library.

Profile. An outline drawing representing a vertical section of land, water, underlying strata, etc., generally with the vertical scale exaggerated.

Program Dissertation. A dissertation accompanying a "program" (*i.e.,* announcement of a memorial exercise, lecture, etc.) published by a university or school, especially one in Germany, Austria, Switzerland, or one of the Scandinavian countries. [Ca.]

Prohibited Book. *See* Banned Book; Index Librorum Prohibitorum.

Projection. The method employed by a cartographer for representing on a plane the whole or a part of the earth's surface.

Projection Bulb. A lamp used in a projector, having a very compact filament to approximate a point source of light. [M.]

Projection Distance. The distance from the objective to the screen on which the image is in focus. Often called Throw. [M.]

Projection Head. The projector incorporated in a reading machine. [M.]

Projection Lens. *See* Objective. [M.]

Projection Print. *See* Enlargement. [M.]

Projection Printing. *See* Enlarging. [M.]

Projection Ratio. The ratio of the projected image on the screen to the image on the film. [M.]

Projector. An optical device consist-ing of a light source, lens system, and image holder, for projecting the image on a screen. Also called Film Projector. [M.]

Prompt Copy. *See* Promptbook.

Promptbook. The copy of a play used by a prompter, showing action of the play, cues, movements of actors, properties, costume, and scene and light plots. Also known as Prompt Copy.

Proof. 1. A preliminary impression from composed type for examination and correction. Sometimes called Proof Sheet. 2. A preliminary impression from an engraved plate or block, or a lithographic stone. Usually called Trial Proof. 3. An impression from a finished plate taken before the regular impression is published and usually before the title or other inscription is added. Sometimes called Proof Print and Proof Impression.

Proof (Binding). *See* Binding Proof.

Proof, Artist's. *See* Artist's Proof.

Proof, Author's. *See* Author's Proof.

Proof, Galley. *See* Galley Proof.

Proof, Lettered. *See* Lettered Proof.

Proof, Open-letter. *See* Open-letter Proof.

Proof, Page. *See* Page Proof.

Proof, Remarque. *See* Artist's Proof.

Proof Before Letters. A proof of an engraving without any inscription, *i.e.,* before title and names of artist and engraver are supplied.

Proof Impression. *See* Proof (3).

Proof in Slips. *See* Galley Proof.

Proof Print. *See* Proof (3).

Proof Sheet. *See* Proof (1).

Proofsheet Depository. A library that receives free from the Library of Congress a complete set of all its cards printed before proofsheets of cards were issued, to supplement a full collection of proofsheets.

Proprietary Library. A library owned by shareholders who acquire shares in the ownership of the library by purchase or gift. The use of the library is generally confined to shareholders or to persons designated by them.

Prospectus. 1. A pamphlet or folder issued by a publisher to announce a work newly published or to be published, sometimes including sample pages. 2. A book containing sample pages and specimens of text, illustrations, and style of binding of a publication, for use in soliciting orders.

Provenance. The source, history of transmission or ownership, as of a book or manuscript.

Provisional Edition. A tentative edition preceding a final edition that may incorporate additions and changes.

Pseudonym. A false name assumed by an author to conceal his identity. [C.]

Public Catalog. A card catalog for public use as distinguished from one limited to official use.

Public Document. *See* Document; Government Publication.

Public Library. 1. A library that serves free all residents of a community, district, or region, and receives its financial support, in whole or in part, from public funds. 2. Earlier, a library accessible to all residents of a community, but not generally free, as distinguished from a private library; *e.g.*, a society library, a subscription library.

Publication Date. 1. The year in which a book is published, generally the date given at the bottom of the title page, in distinction from copyright and other dates. Also known as Date of Publication. 2. The day of the month or week on which a periodical is issued. Also known as Publication Day. 3. The month and day when a new book is placed on sale by a publisher, generally announced in advance. Also known as Publication Day and Date of Publication.

Publication Day. *See* Publication Date (2, 3).

Publication Exchange. *See* Exchange (1).

Publication Number (Music). *See* Plate Number.

Publication State. *See* State (Engraving).

Publisher. The person, firm, or corporate body undertaking the responsibility for the issue of a book or other printed matter to the public. The same person or firm may be printer, publisher, and bookseller, or printer and publisher, or publisher and bookseller, but since the opening years of the nineteenth century publishing has been, for the most part, a separate business. [C.]

Publisher's Binding. The binding of a book as it is issued by its publisher. It is nearly always identical with edition binding, and commonly implies ordinary cloth.

Publisher's Cover. A case designed for use in an edition binding.

Publisher's Device or Mark. *See* Printer's or Publisher's Mark.

Publisher's Series. A number of books, generally reprints of older, standard, or current books, not necessarily related in subject or treatment, issued by a publisher in uniform style and usually with a common series title, as *Cambridge Edition, Everyman's Library*. Sometimes known as Trade Series and Reprint Series.

Pulp. The mechanically or chemically prepared pasty mixture based on vegetable fibers that is used for making paper.

Pulp Magazine. A twentieth-century type of cheap magazine printed on newsprint and devoted to stories of adventure, mystery, and love. Also known as Pulp-paper Magazine, Pulp Sheet, and Wood-pulp Magazine.

Pulp-paper Magazine. *See* Pulp Magazine.

Pulp Sheet. *See* Pulp Magazine.

Purchasing Agent. *See* Agent.

Pure Notation. A system of notation in which only one kind of symbol is used to indicate the divisions of a classification scheme.

Quad. A shortened form of quadrat, a blank square block of metal lower than height of type, cast in a definite number of ems. Quads are used for indention, spacing, and blank lines.

Quarter Binding. 1. Binding in cloth-covered boards with leather backs, or paper-covered sides with cloth or leather backs, in which the back material extends only slightly on the sides. In quarter binding, the leather (or cloth) back should extend on the boards one eighth the width of the boards. 2. Pamphlet-style library binding (*q.v.*).

Quarter Leather. A quarter binding in which leather is used for the back.

Quarterly. A periodical issued four times a year.

Quarto. 1. Format: a book printed on full-sized sheets folded medially and then transversely, making four leaves or eight pages. 2. Size: according to the American Library Association scale, a book which measures from 25 cm. to 30 cm. in height. [C.]

Quick or Ready Reference. 1. Rapid and easy consultation of material to find information. 2. Reference work limited to the most accessible material.

Quire. (*n.*) Specifically, the one or more sheets or half sheets which comprise a signature, folded and laid together so that the leaves or pages are in proper sequence. Called also Gathering, Section, and Signature. See also In Quires. (*v.*) To lay together two or more folded sheets, one within the other. [Ca.]

Rack. A framework or stand for displaying library books and other material. Also called Display Rack and Exhibit Rack. Distinguished according to use as Book Rack, Magazine Rack, etc.

Radiating or Radial Stack. A stack in which the bookcases are arranged as radii of a semicircle, usually with delivery desk at the center.

Radiation Fin. A fin on a metal lamp house to increase the surface area of the lamp house and correspondingly increase the radiation of heat away from the lamp. [M.]

Rag-content Paper. *See* Rag Paper.

Rag Paper. Paper made entirely or in part from rags. Also known as Rag-content Paper.

Raised Bands. 1. The ridges running across the shelf back of a book that has been sewed on cords. 2. False bands, made to imitate real raised bands.

Range. A double-faced bookcase, one of a series in a stack.

Range Aisle. A narrow passageway between ranges.

Range End. The part of a range which faces the aisle. Also known as Range Front and Stack End.

Range Front. *See* Range End.

Range Guide. A large card, or label, on a range end, to indicate contents of the range.

Range Number. A number assigned to a range to facilitate location of books.

Rare Book. A book so old, scarce, or difficult to find that it seldom appears in the book markets. Among rare books may be included: incunabula, sixteenth- and seventeenth-century imprints, American imprints before 1820, first editions, limited editions, de luxe editions, specially illustrated editions, books in fine bindings, unique copies, books of interest for their associations.

Rare Book Room. *See* Treasure Room.

Readable Book. A book that meets the needs of the layman at the least cost in time and energy; usually nonfiction that presents knowledge as lucidly, simply, and nontechnically as its subject permits.

Reader. 1. A person who uses library material. 2. A member of a special library staff who scans current material to select articles, etc., pertinent to the work of individuals and departments of the organization to be brought to their attention. In a newspaper library, a member of the library staff who scans the several editions of the newspaper and marks the articles for clipping and filing.

Readers' Adviser. A librarian concerned specifically with the reading problems of adults, who recommends books, compiles lists of selected titles, instructs adult readers in the use of the library and its resources, and maintains relations with adult education agencies. Also called Readers' Consultant and Readers' Counselor.

Reader's Card. See Borrower's Card.

Readers' Consultant or Counselor. See Readers' Adviser.

Reader's Note. A descriptive book annotation intended to inform the reader about a book and to interest him in reading it.

Reading Club. 1. A group, with or without formal organization, which meets at specified times under the supervision of a librarian to discuss and review books. 2. A club for school children, generally without meetings, planned to stimulate vacation reading. Also called Summer Reading Club.

Reading Course. A list of books selected for an individual or a group as a guide to systematic, consecutive reading on a definite subject.

Reading Guidance. Directing the choice of books by readers in accordance with their interests and abilities through personal advice or printed lists.

Reading Interests. Topics that appeal to readers, especially to those of the same age, sex, occupation, income, or cultural group.

Reading List. A select, often annotated, list of books, or of books and articles, suggested for reading and study. Also known as Reference List and Reference Reading List.

Reading Machine. An apparatus consisting essentially of a projector and a screen, either opaque or translucent, on which microfilm is read. [M.]

Reading Room. A room set apart for reading and study, usually provided with books or other material.

Reading Shelves. Checking of shelves to see that books are in correct order. Also known as Revising Shelves and Shelf Reading.

Ready Reference. See Quick or Ready Reference.

Rear Projection Screen. A screen on which the image is projected from the rear, the image being viewed from the front. [M.]

Reback. To put a new shelf back on a volume without any other rebinding.

Rebind. (n.) A volume that has been rebound. (v.) To subject a volume to rebinding.

Rebinding. The thorough rehabilitation of a worn book, the minimum of work done being resewing and putting on a new cover.

Recall. (n.) A request by a library for the return of a borrowed book when another reader needs it. (v.) To request a borrower to return a book needed by another reader.

Recasing. 1. The replacing (resetting)

of the cover on a volume that has come out of its cover or has loosened in the cover, the sewing and the cover being still in good condition. 2. The same process, except that the volume is resewn and/or provided with new end papers. 3. The covering of a volume with a new case or new cover.

Receiving Desk. *See* Circulation Desk.

Receiving Room. *See* Shipping Room.

Recension. 1. A textual revision of a work, based on critical study of earlier texts and sources. 2. A text thus established by critical revision.

Reconditioning (of film). The process of restoring old film to a usable condition by cleaning, rehumidifying, and reviving its pliableness. [M.]

Reconstructed Binding. A trade name for the binding on a pre-library-bound book when the volume is resewed and put back into the original publisher's cover.

Record Group. A single organized and identified body of records constituting usually the archives (or the part thereof in the custody of an archival establishment) of an autonomous record-keeping agency or establishment.

Re-covering. The process of making a new cover and attaching it to a volume.

Recreational Reading. Any kind of reading matter read for diversion in distinction from that read in connection with work or study.

Recto. The right-hand page of an open book, usually bearing the odd page number. Also, the front of a separate printed sheet, *e.g.*, of a broadside. Formerly called Folio Recto. [C.]

Red Book. 1. A book containing an official list of state employees. 2. An official peerage list.

Red Rope. *See* Manila Rope.

Red Under Gold. Having edges, and sometimes decoration, colored red and then gilded.

Reduction Ratio. The ratio of the size of the original material to the size of the photographic image. [M.]

Reel. 1. A flanged spool on which film is wound. Also called Film Spool. 2. The quantity of film that can be wound on such a spool. [M.]

Reference. A direction from one heading to another. [C.]

Reference Book. 1. A book designed by its arrangement and treatment to be consulted for definite items of information rather than to be read consecutively. 2. A book whose use is restricted to the library building.

Reference Card. A catalog card bearing a cross reference.

Reference Card or Slip. (Special libraries). *See* Search Record.

Reference Collection. A collection of books and other materials in a library useful for supplying information, kept together for convenience and generally not allowed to circulate.

Reference Department. 1. The part of a library in which its reference books are kept for consultation. 2. The administrative unit in charge of the reference work of a library.

Reference Librarian. 1. A librarian in charge of the work of a reference department. For a department of two or more the terms Chief of Reference Department and Chief Reference Librarian are coming into use and are to be preferred. *Cf.* Chief. 2. A professional assistant in a reference department, as senior reference librarian.

Reference Library. 1. A library with either a general collection or a collection limited to a special field, organized for consultation and research, and generally noncirculating. 2. A library whose books may not be taken from the building.

Reference List. *See* Reading List.

Reference Mark. A symbol, letter, or figure used in printing to refer to material in another place, as in a footnote. Symbols in order of use are: * (asterisk), † (dagger), ‡ (double dagger), § (section mark), ‖ (parallels), ¶ (paragraph mark).

Reference Matter. One of the three main parts of a book, that containing notes, bibliography, appendixes, indexes, etc. Sometimes called Subsidiaries.

Reference Reading List. *See* Reading List.

Reference Slip. *See* Search Record.

Reference Work. 1. That phase of library work which is directly concerned with assistance to readers in securing information and in using the resources of the library in study and research. 2. The work of a reference department.

Reflection Copying. *See* Contact Printing. [M.]

Reflex Copying. *See* Contact Printing. [M.]

Regional Branch. A larger branch library which acts as a reference and administrative center for a group of smaller branches in a public library system.

Regional Catalog. A union catalog of libraries and collections in a particular locality or section, such as a metropolitan area, a state, or a group of states. Also called Regional Union Catalog.

Regional Document Library. A library in a particular area that is responsible for collecting federal government documents and local government documents of the section, for the use of all libraries in the area.

Regional Library. A public library serving a group of communities, or several counties, and supported in whole or in part by public funds from the governmental units served. Sometimes known as District Library.

Regional Union Catalog. *See* Regional Catalog; Union Catalog (1).

Register. 1. The series of symbols by which the leaves of the signatures are marked to indicate their order to the folder and the binder. [C.] 2. Registrum (*q.v.*). 3. Adjustment of printing so that lines or columns of print on both sides of a leaf exactly correspond, or, in multicolor work, so that the successive impressions are in exactly correct relation to each other. 4. A ribbon attached to a book for marking a place. Also called Bookmark, Marker, Ribbon, and Ribbon Marker. 5. A list or official roster.

Registration. The enrollment of persons wishing to borrow books from a library.

Registration Card. A card that records a borrower's name and his borrower's number.

Registration Department. The administrative unit that handles the registration of borrowers and the related records.

Registration File. *See* Application File; Registration Record or File.

Registration Record or File. An alphabetical or a numerical list of library borrowers. Also called Borrowers' File, Borrowers' Register.

Registrum or Register. A list of the quires, often given at the end of early printed books (especially those printed in Italy) to aid the binder in assembling and arranging a complete copy. The list may consist of the catchwords, the signature marks, or a combination of the two. [C.]

Reinforced Binding. 1. An inadequate term for pre-library binding. *See* Pre-library-bound. 2. A term loosely used by publishers for an edition binding that purports to be sufficiently strengthened to withstand hard library use.

Reinforced Library Binding. A secondary binding in pre-library-bound style. (Properly used only to refer to Class "A" pre-library binding, but sometimes used in referring to a prebound book in which the publisher's original cover is retained.)

Reissue. *See* Issue (Edition, etc.).

Relation. An English nonperiodic pamphlet describing a battle or some other event, a forerunner of the newspaper. Also known as a "discourse" or a "narration."

Relative Index. An index to a classification scheme which shows all phases and relations of each subject.

Relative Location. The arrangement of books in a library according to their relations to each other, allowing the introduction of new material in its proper relation to material on the shelves. Contrasted with Fixed Location. Also known as Movable Location.

Release. *See* Press Release.

Relief Map. A type of map that represents elevations and depressions of the surface of the earth by various methods.

Relief Printing. Printing from raised surfaces, as from type, in distinction from intaglio printing and planographic printing.

Remainder. A publisher's stock of unsold copies of a book disposed of as a lot, to be resold at a reduced price.

Remarque Proof. *See* Artist's Proof.

Remedial Reading. Reading designed to help readers overcome disabilities due to lack of educational opportunities, physical handicaps, or retarded mentality, so that they may be able to read with greater ease and with clearer understanding.

Renewal. 1. Recharging of books to the same borrower at expiration of period of loan. 2. The reregistration of a borrower. Sometimes restricted to immediate reissue of a borrower's card after expiration of his old card.

Renewal Slip. A form on which is recorded information necessary for the renewal of a book loan.

Rental Card. 1. A special borrower's card on which loans from a rental collection are recorded. 2. A special book card for a book in a rental collection.

Rental Collection. A group of selected books that are circulated for a small fee. Sometimes called Rental Library. If the books are duplicates of books in the regular library collection, the terms Duplicate Pay Collection and Pay Duplicate Collection are also used.

Rental Library. 1. A library owned by a commercial agency which charges a small fee for books loaned. 2. Sometimes, a rental collection (*q.v.*).

Repair Department. The administrative unit that has charge of the mending of books when rebinding is not necessary, the placing of pamphlets in binders, and similar work. Also known as Book Repair Department.

Repairing. The partial rehabilitation of a worn book, the amount of work done being less than the minimum involved in rebinding and more than the maximum involved in mending. Includes such operations as restoring cover and reinforcing at joints. Not to be confused with mending.

Repertory Catalog. *See* Union Catalog.

Replacement. 1. The substitution of another copy of a title or volume for one no longer in a library. 2. The copy of a title or volume substituted, or to be substituted, for another copy no longer in a library.

Report. 1. A publication giving an official or formal record, as of some special investigation, of the activities of a corporate body, of the proceedings of a legislative assembly. 2. *Pl.* Publications giving judicial opinions or decisions.

Report Writing. In a special library, presenting in written form the results of a search for information asked for, especially when pertinent information exists in many publications but the amount in each is limited, and when information is gathered by correspondence, telephone, and interview.

Reprint. A new printing, without material alteration, from new or original type or plates, as distinguished from copies made by typing, or reproductions made by a mechanical or a photomechanical process. Prefer the specific terms, Edition, Impression, Issue, Offprint, etc. A textual reprint is one whose text follows exactly that of a particular edition. [C.]

Reprint Edition. A cheap edition of a standard work or of a popular copyrighted work, from plates used in the regular trade edition, usually issued through agreement with the original publisher.

Reprint Series. *See* Publisher's Series.

Republication. 1. A reissuing of a work by a different publisher without change in text. Sometimes applied to a reprinting in another country. 2. A work thus reissued. 3. In a very broad sense, a reissuing of a work, with or without change in text, or as a new edition; a work thus reissued.

Request Form. A form distributed to the clientele of a special organization library and used to request information or material from the library.

Required Reading Room. *See* Reserved Book Department (1).

Reregistration, Continuous. *See* Continuous Reregistration.

Rescript. *See* Palimpsest.

Research Book. In motion-picture research libraries, a scrapbook made up of abstracts and reference material relating to the setting, architecture, costume, etc., collected for a particular picture in advance, or in course, of production.

Research Librarian. 1. A member of a university library staff, holding one of the positions established experimentally by the Carnegie Corporation, who devotes his time to assisting faculty members in their research, the results of which are to be published. 2. In a special library, a librarian whose primary function is to collect information and material from within and without the organization, from written sources, and from individuals and organizations that are authorities in certain fields. The research librarian may or may not summarize and appraise, in report form, the information gathered.

Research Library. A reference library provided with specialized material, where exhaustive investigation can be carried on, in a particular field, as in a technological library, or in several fields, as in a university library.

Research or Search Service. Service rendered by special librarians through examination, appraisal, and summarizing of information gathered from written sources and from individuals and organizations that are authorities in specific fields. It is not to be confused with creative or scientific research.

Reserve Card. A form on which a patron files a request for a book to be held for him when it is available.

Reserve Collection. Branch library material not in active use stored at a central location and available for all agencies upon request.

Reserved Book. 1. A book held for a borrower a certain length of time in response to his request. 2. One of a group of books segregated and withheld from general circulation, particularly those needed for college or school required reading.

Reserved Book Collection. A collection of material segregated and restricted in circulation, especially in a college or a university library.

Reserved Book Department. 1. The part of a college or a university library where books for required reading are segregated. Sometimes called Required Reading Room and Assigned Reading Room. 2. The section of a college or university library staff in charge of reserved books.

Reservoir Library. *See* Deposit Library.

Residence Hall Library. *See* Dormitory Library.

Residual Hypo. Hypo that remains in the film after the film has been processed; it is detrimental to the life of the film. [M.]

Resolution. *See* Resolving Power. [M.]

Resolving Power. 1. The ability of a lens to give a sharp image for a given aperture. 2. The ability of a film to record a sharp image. [M.]

Restricted Book. A book whose circulation is limited purposely, usually because of special demand, its reference value, costliness, rarity, or questionable moral tone.

Restricted Circulation. The issuing

of certain material with some limitation, as on period of loan, number of books, or persons allowed to borrow it.

Résumé. A summary of the chief points of a work.

Return Desk. *See* Circulation Desk.

Reversal Process. A process of development that produces a positive instead of a negative image from the originally exposed film. [M.]

Review. 1. An evaluation of a literary work, usually published in a periodical or a newspaper. 2. A periodical publication primarily devoted to critical articles and reviews of new books.

Review Copy. A copy of a new book sent free by a publisher for review purposes.

Revised Braille. In England, a revision of the English braille introduced in 1905. In the United States, braille, grade one and a half, was originally called revised braille, grade one and a half. *Obsolete.*

Revised Edition. A new edition with the text of the original edition changed and corrected, and sometimes with additions that supplement it or bring it up to date.

Revised Impression. *See* Issue (Edition, etc.).

Reviser. 1. A cataloger who checks and corrects work in process, such as assignment of classification numbers and preparation of catalog entries. 2. An assistant in a library school who checks and corrects the written work of students, particularly in courses in cataloging and classification, and often in reference work and book selection.

Revising Shelves. *See* Reading Shelves.

Revolving Bookcase. A compact kind of bookcase having four faces of one or more tiers built around a central cylinder that turns on a spindle.

Rewind. An apparatus consisting of two spindles geared to cranks for the unwinding and rewinding of reels of film. [M.]

Ribbon. *See* Bookmark; Register (4).

Ribbon Arrangement. A method of shelving books with nonfiction on upper shelves and fiction on lower shelves, or vice versa, or with fiction on middle shelves and nonfiction on upper and lower shelves.

Ribbon Marker. *See* Bookmark; Register (4).

Ridge. *See* Flange.

Ring Binding. An old style of mechanical binding, involving the use of several metal rings.

Roan. Sheepskin dyed a dark color and having an irregular surface.

Roll. An early form of book that was written on a strip of papyrus or other material and rolled on a rod or rods. Also called Rolled Book and Scroll.

Rolled Book. *See* Roll.

Rolled Edges. Edges of book covers decorated with a roll, or "roulette," a finishing tool having a brass wheel with a design on its rim.

Roller Shelves. Large shelves for storing folios, etc., fitted with a series of small rollers to facilitate the handling of the books and to protect the bindings.

Rolling Press. A single- or a double-faced movable bookcase, suspended from overhead tracks or running on floor tracks, which slides between the ranges of a stack. Also known as Hanging Press.

Roman à Clef. A novel in which one or more characters are based on real people, with names disguised.

Roman Type. 1. An early Italian type based on capitals in Latin inscriptions and small letters in humanistic script. 2. Styles of type now commonly used for books, periodicals, and newspapers, characterized by serifs and upright strokes heavier than horizontal strokes, as distinguished from black letter and italic. Also called Modern Roman.

Rotogravure. 1. An intaglio process of printing pictures, a modification of photogravure, in which the image is reproduced on a copper cylinder, or a copper plate to be attached to a cylinder, for printing on a rotary press. 2. A print or an illustration produced by this process.

Rough Edges. A generic term, including "uncut (untrimmed) edges" and "deckle edges."

Round Brackets. *See* Curves.

Round or Rounded Corner. 1. Library corner (*q.v.*). 2. A book cover in which the board is cut off at the corner before covering is added; usually confined to leather bindings.

Routine Slip. *See* Process Slip.

Routing. The systematic circulating of material to staff members; or, in a special organization library, the circulating of new publications among members of its clientele in accordance with their work interests or fields of specialization.

Routing, Automatic. *See* Automatic Routing.

Routing, Selective. *See* Selective Routing.

Routing Form. *See* Routing Slip or Form.

Routing Slip or Form. A form attached in a library to a periodical or other publication which is to be sent to one or more persons, generally with spaces for names, dates, etc.

Rub. *See* Rub-off.

Rub-off. An impression of the lettering on the back of a book, made by placing a piece of strong, thin paper over the back, and rubbing it with the lead of a heavy pencil or something similar; used for matching bindings. Also called Rubbing and Rub.

Rubbing. *See* Rub-off.

Rubricated. Having initials, catchwords, titles, or other parts of a work written or printed in red, and sometimes blue or other colors, as in ancient manuscripts and early printed books.

Rudolph Continuous Indexer. A cabinet for storing catalog entries, in which the entries are inserted in a series of pressboard leaves which revolve around a pair of hexagonal drums. Practically obsolete.

Rule Mark or Ruled Line. In early manuscripts, one of the vertical or parallel horizontal lines made to guide the transcriber in making an accurate and attractive copy.

Rune. Any letter or character of the early alphabet used by the Teutonic or Germanic peoples.

Runner. *See* Page (2).

Running Head. A line of printing at the top of each page of a book, giving the title of the work, the chapter title, or the subject of the chapter or page.

Running Title. A title of the book repeated at the head (or the foot) of the pages, not necessarily on both versos and rectos. *Cf.* Headline, Caption Title. [C.]

Russia. A fine calf, of a special tannage, finished with birch oil, which gives it a characteristic spicy odor.

Russia Cowhide. *See* American Russia.

Rustic Capital. A lighter and less formal capital than the square capital; used in early manuscripts.

Saddle Stitching. Stitching together leaves (double leaves inserted one within the other) with thread or wire passing through the bulk of the volume at the fold line. So called from the saddle of a stitching machine. *Cf.* Side Stitching.

Safety Film. *See* Cellulose Acetate. [M.]

Sample Back. A strip of binding material made up like the backstrip of a book, to be used as a sample for matching color, fabric, lettering, etc.

Sans-serif. A simple outline style of type having even strokes and no cross bars at ends of strokes. Also called Block Letter, Printers' Gothic, and by American printers, Gothic. In England also known as Doric and Grotesque.

Scale. The ratio between a given distance on a map to the corresponding distance on the earth's surface.

Scan. In a special library, to examine periodical and other material and evaluate the usefulness of the information it contains to the library's clientele, or more specifically to the activities of individuals served by the library.

Scanning Device. An attachment on some reading machines that permits the reader to bring to or near the center of the screen the section of the image that he is reading. [M.]

Scheme of Service. *See* Graded Scheme of Service.

School Branch Library. A library agency in a school building, administered by a public library and/or a board of education for the use of students and teachers, and frequently for adults of the neighborhood.

School Department. *See* School Libraries Department (1).

School Deposit. *See* Classroom Library (1); Classroom Loan.

School District Library. 1. Earlier, a tax-supported library established in a school district for the use of schools and free to all residents of the district. Also called District Library. 2. A free public library established and financially supported by action of a school district for the use of all residents of the district, and supervised by a local board of education or by a separate library board.

School Duplicate Collection. A collection of books for boys and girls of elementary and junior high school age, duplicating books in a children's department and used to supply books for schoolroom use.

School Librarian. A professionally trained librarian in charge of a school library.

School Libraries Department. 1. The administrative unit of a public library that supervises libraries in schools and/or has charge of the distribution of books and other reading matter to schools. Also called School Department and Schools Department. 2. The section of a board of education responsible for the activities of school libraries in a school system.

School Library. 1. An organized collection of books housed in a school for the use of students and teachers, and in charge of a librarian or a teacher. 2. In a university, a collection of books related to the work of a particular school or college, administered separately by the school or college or as a part of the university library.

School Library Supervisor. A member of the staff of a library or a local or state board of education who inspects school libraries and advises and directs the school librarians.

School Loan. *See* Classroom Library (1); Classroom Loan.

Schoolroom Library. *See* Classroom Library (1).

Schools Department. *See* School Libraries Department (1).

Schrotblatt. *See* Dotted Print.

Schwabacher. 1. An early variety of Gothic type used in Germany. 2. A type used in Germany today, based on early Gothic designs.

Scintillation. The phenomenon of myriad small points of light and spectra produced by some translucent screens. [M.]

Score. The written, or printed form of a musical work in which the music for the participating voices and or instruments appears on two or more staves one above the other.

While the term *score* can be applied to all music that is complete in itself, the term is not usually applied to music for one performer. Music for

keyboard instruments, however, technically falls within the definition given above, for it is generally printed (or written) on two or more staves.

Screen. A specially prepared surface on which an image is projected. [M.]

Screen, Diffusing. *See* Diffusing Screen. [M.]

Screen, Opaque. *See* Opaque Screen. [M.]

Screen, Rear Projection. *See* Rear Projection Screen. [M.]

Screen, Translucent. *See* Translucent Screen. [M.]

Screen Image. The projected image that appears on a screen. [M.]

Scribal Copy. A written manuscript, produced by a copyist, as opposed to the original manuscript produced by the author himself or from his dictation.

Scrinium. A cylinder-shaped receptacle with movable top used by the Romans to hold a number of scrolls.

Script. 1. A typescript; specifically, a typescript of a play, a motion-picture play, the text of the spoken part of a radio program, etc. 2. A type style that resembles handwriting.

Scriptorium. Literally, a writing room. A place in a medieval monastery or abbey set apart for the preparation of manuscripts.

Scroll. *See* Roll.

Seal. A bookbinding leather derived from the Greenland or Newfoundland seal; generally used for limp bindings.

Seal Print. A fifteenth-century woodcut which has received blind embossing of the paper after the print has been made. Sometimes called Gypsographic Print.

Sealskin. *See* Seal.

Search Procedure. The plan of search used in a particular special library or class of special libraries, especially for certain types or categories of information searches.

Search Record. A record in a special library which shows the publications, individuals, and organizations consulted in an extended search for information. The record card is called a Reference Card or a Reference Slip.

Search Service. *See* Research or Search Service; Literature Search.

"Second" Indention. The distance from the left edge of a catalog card at which, according to predetermined rules, the title normally begins; on a standard ruled card, at the second vertical line. Also called Inner Indention, Title Indention, and Paragraph Indention. [Ca.]

Secondary Entry. *See* Added Entry.

Secondary Fulness. The use of an abbreviated form of an author's name for secondary entries in a catalog when the unit card is not used. Also known as Author Abbreviation and Subject Fulness.

Secondary Sources. Any material other than primary sources used in the preparation of a written work.

Section. 1. One of the separate parts that together make up a whole, as a section of a bookcase or of a card catalog cabinet. 2. A tier (*q.v.*). 3. A subdivision of an administrative unit in a library; occasionally, the larger administrative unit. Sometimes called Division or Department. 4. In the Decimal classification, one of the subdivisions of a division. 5. A quire (*q.v.*). 6. One of the distinctive parts in which a newspaper is sometimes issued, *e.g.*, financial section.

Section Title. *See* Half Title (2).

Sectional Title. *See* Half Title (2).

"See Also" Cross Reference. *See* "See Also" Reference.

"See Also" Reference. A direction in a catalog from a term or name under which entries are listed to another term or name under which additional or allied information may be found.

"See" Cross Reference. *See* "See" Reference.

"See" Reference. A direction in a catalog from a term or name under which no entries are listed to a term or name under which entries are listed. Other terms used are: "See" Cross Reference, "See" Subject Reference, "See" Card and "See" Reference Card.

Selection Division. The section of an acquisition department or an order department that handles the selection of books.

Selective Cataloging. The cataloging of certain types of material in a library with either shorter or fuller cataloging than that used for the bulk of the library collection.

Selective Routing. In a special library, a plan whereby articles and publications are sent to individual members of the organization served by the library on the basis of their specific work interests.

Self-charging System. Any method of recording book loans in which the borrower assists in making the record.

Self-cover. A pamphlet cover made of the same paper as the body of the pamphlet.

Semé (Semée). Characterized by semis. Also known as Powdered.

Seminar Room. 1. A small room in a college or a university library in which selected material on a subject is placed temporarily for the use of a group engaged in special research. 2. A room in a college or a university library in which a large part of its collection in a particular field is shelved for the convenience of advanced students and faculty.

Semis. A binding decoration of small figures, such as sprays, flowers, and leaves, repeated frequently at regular intervals, over the greater portion of the binding, thus producing a powdered or sprinkled effect.

Senior. A personnel rating term added to titles of positions to indicate relative rank; applied usually to assistants who under supervision do the more difficult nonsupervisory work, or subject to administrative authorization and approval are responsible for particular types of work requiring special qualifications.

Senior Undergraduate Library School. A school for education in librarianship that met minimum standards of the Board of Education for Librarianship of the American Library Association from 1925 to 1933 by being connected with a degree-conferring institution, requiring for entrance three years of college work, and meeting requirements with respect to faculty, curriculum, and other factors. *Cf.* Type III Library School.

Sensitivity. A relative measure of the rate of change which takes place in the photochemical substance in the film emulsion when exposed to various or all of the wave lengths of the spectrum at various intensities. Some emulsions are particularly sensitive to certain wave lengths, and a panchromatic emulsion is sensitive to all colors. Also known as Speed of Film. [M.]

Sensitized Paper. Paper coated with a light-sensitive emulsion, generally used for making prints. [M.]

Separate. *See* Offprint.

Separate Registration. A method of recording applicants for borrowers' cards in which each branch records its own borrowers and no combined record of borrowers is kept at the central library.

Sequel. A work, complete in itself, that continues a narrative from an earlier work.

Serial. 1. A publication issued in successive parts, usually at regular intervals, and, as a rule, intended to be continued indefinitely. Serials include periodicals, annuals (reports, yearbooks, etc.) and memoirs, proceedings, and transactions of societies. [C.] 2. Any literary composition, especially a novel, published in consecutive numbers of a periodical.

Serial Catalog. A public or an official catalog of serials in a library, with a record of the library's holdings.

Serial Number. 1. The number denoting the place of a publication in a series, as no. 42, Monograph 6. [Ca.] 2. One of the consecutive numbers sometimes assigned to entries in a bibliography or a printed catalog. 3. A card number (*q.v.*). 4. One of the consecutive numbers assigned to a volume of the Congressional set of United States government publications.

Serial Record. A record of the serial holdings of a library.

Serial Section. A division of an order or an acquisition department that has charge of the acquisition of serials; or a subdivision of a preparation division in charge of the cataloging of serials.

Serial Set. *See* Congressional Edition.

Serials Department. The administrative unit in charge of handling serials, which may include ordering, checking, cataloging, preparation for binding, etc.

Series. 1. A number of separate works, usually related to one another in subject or otherwise, issued in succession, normally by the same publisher and in uniform style, with a collective title which generally appears at the head of the title page, on the half title, or on the cover. 2. Each of two or more volumes of essays, lectures, articles, or other writings, similar in character and issued in sequence, *e.g.,* Lowell's *Among my books,* second series. 3. Several successive volumes of a periodical or other serial publication numbered separately in order to distinguish them from preceding or following volumes of the same publication, *e.g.,* Notes and queries, 1st series, 2d series, etc. [C.]

Series (Archives). A group of documents of uniform character systematically organized or filed as a unit and intended to be kept together in a definite arrangement.

Series Entry. In a catalog, an entry, usually brief, of the several works in the library which belong to a series under the name of the series as a heading; in a bibliography, either a partial or a complete list of the works in a series. [Ca.]

Series Note. In a catalog or a bibliography, a note stating the name of a series to which a book belongs. The series note ordinarily follows the collation. [Ca.]

Series Title. The name of the series to which a book belongs, indicated on the cover, title page, or somewhere else in the book.

Serif. A short, fine line crossing or projecting from the main stroke of a letter as a finish, one of the main elements in determining specific type styles.

Service. 1. An agency which supplies information, especially current data, in easily available form, not readily available otherwise. The information may be issued in printed, multigraphed, loose-leaf, or other form, and may be supplied regularly and or on request. 2. The information supplied in this way.

Service Basis. A method of scaling prices for a publication, determined by such criteria as total income, book fund, circulation, and potential value of the publication to a subscriber; for periodical indexes, based on number of indexed periodicals in a library.

Service Department. 1. Any administrative unit of a library in which direct contact is made with patrons. 2. In some libraries, an administrative unit that combines the functions of circulation and reference departments.

Session Laws. Publications containing collections of laws passed by a state legislature or, formerly, of laws passed during particular sessions of Congress. The federal session laws, which were slip laws collected and reprinted with different page numbers, were also known as Pamphlet Laws.

Set. A series associated by common authorship or publication. Specifically, a collection of books forming a unit, as the works of one author issued in uniform style, a file of periodicals, related works on a particular subject, or unrelated books printed uniformly and intended to be sold as a group; as, a *set* of Dickens; a *set* of works on sociology. [By permission; from Webster's *New International Dictionary*, Second Edition, copyright, 1934, 1939, by G. & C. Merriam Co.]

Set-solid. Without leading between lines of type.

Setoff. *See* Offset (1).

Sewed. 1. Of, or pertaining to, a volume in which the sewing has been complete. 2. Of, or pertaining to, a temporary binding, without covers, and with only enough sewing or stitching to hold the pages together until the volume is fully bound. The term is used almost exclusively with reference to pamphlets, brochures, and books of foreign origin.

Sewing. In bookbinding, fastening sections together one at a time by means of a needle and thread, until the volume is completed. To be distinguished from Stitching.

Sewing Through the Fold. *See* Fold Sewing.

Shareholders' Library. *See* Proprietary Library.

Sharpness. The clearness or distinctness of either an optical or a photographic image. [M.]

Sheaf Catalog. A catalog formed by sheets, slips, or cards fastened in a binder that permits the insertion of new material; used chiefly in English libraries.

Sheep. Leather made from sheepskin.

Sheep-bound Set. *See* Congressional Edition.

Sheepskin. *See* Sheep.

Sheet. 1. One of the separate pieces of definite size in which paper is made. 2. Such a sheet printed so that it may be folded to form consecutive pages for a book or pamphlet of a required size. See also In Sheets. 3. As used in collation, a separate sheet of any size printed to be read unfolded, *i.e.*, with text or illustration imposed as a single page on one side or on each side of the paper. [Ca.]

Sheet Microfilm. A sheet of film on which there are many frames of microphotographs in a rectangular pattern. [M.]

Shelf. A long, flat, horizontal piece of wood or other material, solid or fabricated, attached to and supported by a wall or two uprights.

Shelf Back. *See* Backbone.

Shelf Capacity. The capacity of a library for storing books, generally expressed by the total number of books which can be accommodated on the shelves. Also called Book Capacity. *Cf.* Stack Capacity.

Shelf Department. The administrative unit in charge of the care of books on the shelves, and sometimes of other work, such as classification, shelf-listing, and inventory.

Shelf Height. The distance between shelves adopted arbitrarily by a library to accommodate books of a certain size, as octavos, quartos, folios.

Shelf Label. A small label to fit on an individual shelf.

Shelf List. A record of the books in a library arranged in the order in which they stand on the shelves.

Shelf Mark. 1. In fixed location, a letter or number indicating the location of a special shelf. 2. A call number (*q.v.*).

Shelf Number. The number assigned to a shelf in a fixed location system.

Shelf Reading. *See* Reading Shelves.

Shelf Support. The part of a stack structure that holds the shelves; directly, as in a standard stack, or indirectly, as in a bracket stack.

Shelf Upright. *See* Stack Column.

Shelving. 1. Collectively, the shelves upon which books and other material are stored. 2. The act of placing books on library shelves in proper order.

Shipping Room. The section of a library in which material is received and sorted, and material to be sent to other libraries, branches, or departments is prepared for shipment or transfer. Sometimes known as Receiving Room, or Receiving and Shipping Room.

Short Form Cataloging. The use of shortened forms in certain types of entries, as, for example, the omission or condensation of certain items of information in a title entry.

Shorts. Books delayed in shipment because not in dealer's stock when order is received.

Shoulder. *See* Flange.

Shoulder Head. *See* Shoulder Note.

Shoulder Note. A note at the upper and outer corner of a page. Also called Shoulder Head.

Shutter. An automatic mechanism designed to allow light to pass through the lens to the sensitized material for a definite period of time to make an exposure. [M.]

Shutter Speed. The time of an exposure. [M.]

Side. 1. The front or back cover face of a bound book. 2. The paper, cloth, or other material used on the side of a cover. Also called Siding.

Side Heading. *See* Sidehead or Side Heading.

Side Stitching. Stitching together single leaves or sections near the binding edge, with thread or wire, from front to back through the entire thickness of the leaves or sections. Distinguished from Saddle Stitching. Also called Flat Sewing and Flat Stitching.

Side Title. A title impressed on the front cover of a bound book.

Side-wire. In pamphlet binding, to side-stitch with wire staples.

Sidehead or Side Heading. A heading at the side of printed matter on a page, often set in on the same line with the beginning of a paragraph.

Sidenote. *See* Marginal Note.

Siding. *See* Side (2).

Signature. 1. A distinguishing mark, letter or number, or some combination of these, placed usually at the foot of the first page of each quire of a book or pamphlet to indicate its order to the folder and the binder.

The letters J, V, and W are ordinarily omitted, following the general practice in manuscripts and early printed books of using the Latin alphabet in which I stands for both I and J, V for both U and V, and there is no W.

When the quire includes additional sheets or a portion of a sheet (Inset) these also are signed to indicate how they are to be folded and inserted. In former times, the signature mark (or signature letter) was frequently given on several leaves at the beginning of the quire thus: A, Aii, Aiii, etc.

2. The printed sheet or sheets so marked, whether unfolded, or folded and quired. [C.]

Signature Title. An abbreviated form of the title of a book, given on the same line as the signature, but toward the inner margin of the first leaf of a gathering.

Silking. A process for repairing or preserving paper by the application of silk chiffon to one or both sides of the paper.

Silvered. Of book edges, treated with silver instead of gold.

Single-entry Charging System. A method of recording book loans in which only one record is kept, *e.g.,* a book record. Also called One-card System.

Single-perforate Film. Film that has perforations or sprocket holes on only one edge. [M.]

Size (Books). The height of the binding of a book. If the book is of unusual shape, the width also may be given. The fold symbol (format) of a book is loosely used as an indication of its approximate measurement, *e.g.,* f°, 4°, 8°, 12°. [C.] *See also* table in appendix.

Size (Type). *See* Type Size.

Size Card. *See* Cole Size Card.

Size Letters. A series of abbreviations, chiefly single letters, to indicate the sizes of books. Adopted for use of the A.L.A. in 1878. For example: F (folio); Q (quarto).

Size Notation. The method of indicating the size of a book, as by fold symbol, size letter, or measurement in centimeters.

Size Rule. A rule thirty centimeters long on which size letters and corresponding fold symbols are given at proper intervals; used for measuring books.

Skiver. The grain portion of split sheepskin. The term is sometimes extended to include other binding leathers.

Skiver Label. Paper-thin skiver used

for a label, as on an old law book or a public document.

Slide Box. *See* Slipcase.

Slide Case. *See* Slipcase.

Sliding Shelves. Large shelves for the storage of folios, so designed that they may be pulled out from the bookcase in order to facilitate handling of the books and to preserve bindings. *Cf.* Roller Shelves.

Slip. (*n.*) A small strip of paper used for making a note or record, usually designated as call slip, date slip, etc. (*v.*) To discharge a book, taking book card out of the circulation tray and putting it back into the book. Synonym: Card.

Slip (Printing). *See* Galley Proof.

Slip Charging System. A method of recording book loans by means of temporary slips instead of book cards. Also called Slip System.

Slip-in Case. *See* Slipcase.

Slip Law. A law in its first printed form after its passage in Congress.

Slip Proof. *See* Galley Proof.

Slip System. *See* Slip Charging System.

Slipcase. A box designed to protect a book, covering it so that its back only is exposed. Also called Slide Case, Slip-in Case, Open-back Case, and Slide Box. *Cf.* Solander Case.

Slippage. The slipping that sometimes occurs in a continuous printer when the film on which the prints are being made slides along the film from which the printing is being done, or vice versa, resulting in a blurred print. [M.]

Slipping Desk. *See* Circulation Desk.

Sloping Shelves. The lower shelves of a bookcase arranged in a tilted position, so that titles of books can be read more easily. Also called Tilted Shelves.

Small Capital. A capital letter of approximately the same height as a lower-case letter of the same type size. Frequently abbreviated to s.c., or referred to as "small caps."

Small Paper Copy or Edition. A copy, or an edition, of a book printed on paper of smaller size than that used for a large paper edition of the same work.

Smooth Calf. Full-calf binding wholly without tooling.

Sobriquet. A fanciful or humorous appellation given by others; a nickname. [C.]

Social Library. A term formerly rather loosely used for the whole group of proprietary and subscription libraries, including athenaeums, lyceums, young men's associations, mechanics' institutes, mercantile libraries, and similar types.

Society Library. 1. A library established and maintained by an association organized for the purpose, primarily for the use of members but sometimes available to others on payment of fees. 2. A library of specialized material organized for the use of its members by a society interested in a particular subject or field of knowledge.

Society Publication. An official or other publication issued by, or under the auspices of, a society, association, or institution. Occasionally called Association Publication.

Soft-ground Etching. 1. A method of etching that produces the effect of a pencil or crayon drawing by the use of a soft wax etching ground covered with thin transfer paper, on which the drawing is done with a pencil. When the paper is removed it retains bits of the ground, leaving a flecked line. 2. An etching produced by this method.

Solander Case. A book-shaped box for holding a book, pamphlets, or other material, named for its inventor, D. C. Solander. It may open on side or front with hinges, or have two separate parts, one fitting over the other. Also called Solander, Solander Box, and Solander Cover.

Solid. *See* Set-solid.

Sound-recorded Book. *See* Talking Book.

Source Index. A card index to sources of unusual and elusive information, which, in addition to listing publications, may refer to individuals and organizations. More common in special libraries.

Source Material. Fundamental authoritative material relating to a subject, used in the preparation of a later written work, *e.g.*, original records, documents, etc. Also called Original Sources and Primary Sources.

Spanish Americana. All material that has been printed about Spanish America, printed in Spanish America, or written by Spanish Americans, with a frequent restriction of period to that of the formative stage in its history, the final date varying from 1810 to 1824. [Reprinted from Stillwell, *Incunabula and Americana,* by permission of Columbia University Press.]

Special Collection. A collection of material of a certain form, on a certain subject, of a certain period, or gathered together for some particular reason, in a library which is more or less general in character.

Special Edition. 1. An edition of a standard work or the works of a standard author, reissued in a new form, sometimes with introduction, notes, appendix, and illustrations, and generally having a distinctive name. 2. An edition that differs from a regular edition by some distinctive feature, as better paper and binding, or the addition of illustrations. 3. An enlarged issue of a newspaper, usually devoted to a particular subject, as an anniversary number. Also called Special Number (*q.v.*). 4. A library edition (*q.v.*).

Special Editions Collection. A collection of attractive editions of the best known books for children or young people, or of copies of unusual books, generally kept in a special glass case for restricted use.

Special Issue. *See* Special Number.

Special Library. A service organized to make desirable information available to a particular organization or limited group. Its chief functions are: (1) to survey and evaluate current publications, research in progress, and the activities of individual authorities; (2) to organize pertinent written and unwritten information; and (3) to assemble from within and without the library both publications and data, and to disseminate this information, often in abstract or memorandum form, adapted to the individual's work.

Types of special libraries, having various policies, methods, and collections, are: (1) the *special organization library,* serving a corporation, a nonprofit organization, governmental body, etc., and maintained by the organization; (2) the *special branch* of a public library, serving certain occupational groups; (3) the *special subject library,* serving students, professional groups, members, or the general public, on a given subject.

Special Library Edition. *See* Library Edition (2).

Special Number. A single issue or a supplementary section of a serial or a newspaper, devoted to a special subject, with or without serial numbering; *e.g.*, a number of a periodical containing proceedings of a convention, or an anniversary number of a newspaper. Also called Special Issue and, if celebrating an anniversary, Anniversary Issue. A special number of a newspaper is sometimes called Special Edition (*q.v.*).

Special Title Page. A title page, usually with imprint, special to a single part of a larger work, or to a complete work issued or reissued as part of a collection, a series, or a serial publication. [C.]

Specific Cross Reference. *See* Specific Reference.

Specific Entry. Registering a book under a heading which expresses its special subject as distinguished from entering it in a class which includes that subject.

Specific Reference. A reference in a catalog to a particular subject heading or headings, as distinguished from a general reference. Also known as Specific Cross Reference.

Specification Slip. *See* Binding Slip.

Speckled Calf. *See* Sprinkled Calf.

Speed of Film. *See* Sensitivity. [M.]

Spherical Aberration. A blurred image that results when the rays of light that pass through the edges of a lens do not focus at the same point as the rays that pass through the center section of the lens. [M.]

Spine. That part of the cover or binding which conceals the sewed or bound edge of a book, usually bearing the title, and frequently the author. Called also Backbone and Backstrip. [Ca.]
  Catalogers prefer the term Spine.

Spiral Binding. A patented form of binding in which a row of fine holes is drilled through the leaves, trimmed so that each leaf is separate, and a continuous spiral-twisted wire is drawn through the holes. Also known as Coil Binding.

Splicing. The process of cementing two pieces of film together. [M.]

Split Leather. Leather that has been divided into two or more thicknesses.

Spool. A cylinder on which film is wound. [M.]

Spring Back. *See* Loose Back.

Sprinkled Calf. Calf given a speckled appearance by sprinkling with coloring matter or by an acid treatment. Also called Speckled Calf. *Cf.* Mottled Calf.

Sprinkled Edges. Book edges on which color has been irregularly sprinkled or sprayed.

Sprocket Holes. *See* Perforations. [M.]

Spurious Imprint. *See* Fictitious Imprint.

Square. Width exceeding three-fourths of height, as, *square* octavo.

Square Bracket. *See* Bracket.

Square Corner. A book corner in which a piece of the covering material is cut out at the corner so that one turn-in considerably overlaps the other without additional folding.

Squares. The portions of the edges of a book cover that project beyond the paper body of the book.

Stab-stitch. In bookbinding, to stitch with wire or thread, with long stitches, near the back fold and through the entire bulk.

Stack. 1. A permanent self-supporting structure of iron or steel bookcases, extending usually for several stories, and independent of the walls of the building. 2. A series of bookcases, usually double-faced, arranged in a room or in a section of a library for compact storage of the principal book collection in the library. By some librarians the term Book Room is preferred when the bookcases are not an independent steel structure. 3. The room, or the part of a library building, containing a steel or iron stack.

Stack Capacity. The extent of space or volume in a stack, expressed in number of books, square feet of deck area, cubic feet of stack, or cubooks.

Stack Column. The heavy steel framework used in stack construction, which supports the decks and from which shelf supports are suspended.

Stack End. *See* Range End.

Stack Level. *See* Deck.

Stack Permit. A card or slip stating that a person is allowed access to a closed stack.

Stack Supervision. Direction of all work connected with a stack: supplying books requested, returning books to shelves, etc.

Staff. 1. The group of persons who carry on the activities of a library under the direction of the librarian or chief librarian. 2. Occasionally, the group of persons, including the librarian or chief librarian, who carry on the activities of a library. 3. As used with a modifying word or words, a group of persons who carry on the work of a particular department, as circulation staff, catalog department staff; or work of a particular character, as professional staff, clerical staff.

Staff Card. A specially designated borrower's card issued to a staff member.

Staff Code. *See* Staff Manual.

Staff Instruction Book. *See* Staff Manual.

Staff Manual. A guidebook for the staff of a particular library, consisting of rules of procedure in the various departments and branches, and usually containing samples of forms and lists of supplies. Also called Staff Code, Staff Practice Code, Staff Instruction Book. *Cf.* Procedure Manual.

Staff Practice Code. *See* Staff Manual.

Staff Room. A room for staff members, as a rest room, a lunch room, or a room for staff social and recreational purposes.

Stained Calf. 1. Calf that has been stained brown. Calf stained any other color is not referred to as stained calf. 2. Loosely, mottled calf (q.v.).

Stained Edges. Book edges that have been stained with color.

Stained Label. A colored panel printed or painted directly on the binding material as a background for lettering, and simulating a label of leather.

Stained Top. The top edge of a book, stained a uniform color, as distinguished from sprinkled edge, marbled edge, etc.

Stall. *See* Carrel.

Standard Book. A work recognized as of permanent value.

Standard Dot Type. A dot system of embossed type for the blind recommended in the United States in 1913 but never adopted. It combined features of English braille, American braille, and New York point.

Standard English Braille. *See* Braille: Standard English Braille.

Standard Size Card. A card 12.5 x 7 centimeters, now generally used for catalog and other records.

Standard Stack. The type of stack in which the ends of the shelves are supported directly by the standards (the broad upright supports), rather than by brackets in cantilever fashion.

Standard Title. *See* Uniform title.

Standing Order (Continuations). *See* Continuation Order.

Star Map. *See* Chart (3).

Start. 1. A section of leaves that has not been properly secured in the back of a book and hence projects beyond the rest. 2. A break between the signatures of a book, frequently caused by forcing a book open while the leaves are held tightly.

State (Edition). *See* Issue (Edition, etc.).

State (Engraving). An impression from a relatively complete plate, at any stage in the process of perfecting or modifying. The impression may or may not include the title, or the name of the artist or the engraver. The finished state is called the "publication state." An "early impression" is one made while the finished plate is still comparatively new and unworn. [C.]

State (Old maps). An impression that varies from another impression from the same plate because of some change in the plate.

State Document. *See* State Publication.

State Document Center. A library that assumes the responsibility of collecting, organizing, and preserving as complete a file as possible of the public documents of the state in which it is located.

State Library. A library maintained by state funds for the use of state officials, and sometimes for the use of all citizens of the state.

State Library Commission. *See* Library Commission (1).

State Library Extension Agency. An organization created or authorized by a state to promote library service in the state by the establishment, organization, and supervision of public and, sometimes, school libraries, and by the lending of books and other material to libraries and to communities without libraries; *e.g.*, a library commission, a state library.

State Library Organizer. *See* Library Organizer.

State Manual. A publication issued by a state, usually annually or biennially, giving an outline of the state government, lists of officials, and other information. Sometimes called Legislative Manual and Blue Book.

State Publication. Any printed or processed paper, book, periodical, pamphlet, or map, originating in, or printed with the imprint of, or at the expense and by the authority of, any office of a state government. Often called State Document.

Station. *See* Delivery Station; Deposit Station; Page Station.

Stations Division. The section of a branch department that handles books sent to and requests for books from deposit and delivery stations.

Statutes at Large. Statutes in their original full form, particularly, publications containing laws passed during a single session of Congress, together with other documents, such as resolutions, treaties, and presidential proclamations; prior to the law of 1938, issued after each Congress as a consolidation of the session and pamphlet laws.

Steel Engraving. An engraving produced by using a steel plate instead of a copper plate.

Step Printer. A machine for printing film, in which the printing from each frame is made by a separate exposure and not by continuous exposure. [M.]

Stereotype. A plate cast in soft metal from a mold of a printing surface made

of papier mâché or some other substance. Frequently called "stereo."

Stick. A device for holding together the pages of a current issue, or several current issues, of a newspaper, for the convenience of readers. Also known as Newspaper File, Newspaper Rod, and Newspaper Stick.

Stipple Engraving. 1. A kind of engraving that produces light and shade by means of fine dots and short dashes, combining methods of etching and engraving. 2. A print made by this method.

Stippled Edges. The edges of a book that have been spotted irregularly with ink or dye to minimize the showing of dirt.

Stitching. In bookbinding, the fastening together of the leaves by means of thread or wire, each single passage of the threaded needle or wire going through the bulk of the volume. (A generic term, including side stitching and saddle stitching.) To be distinguished from Sewing.

Stop Bath. An acid bath into which films are put after development to stop further developing. [M.]

Stops. *See* Diaphragm. [M.]

Story Hour. A period devoted regularly to the telling or reading of stories to children in the children's department of a public library or in a school library. Also known as Story Half Hour.

Straight-grained Morocco. Morocco in which the natural network grain has been distorted into elongated lines or ridges, all running in the same direction. *Cf.* Hard-grained Morocco.

Straight On. *See* All Along.

Street Index. A list of borrowers arranged according to street addresses.

Strip Film. Film, usually 35 mm. film, in flat strips about ten or twelve inches long. [M.]

Stub. 1. The remaining portion of a leaf cut out of a volume. A cancel is usually mounted on the stub of the canceled leaf. 2. A narrow strip sewed in between sections, for attaching folded maps or other material of extra bulk. Also known as Compensation Guard.

Student Assistant. A student employed part time in the library of a university, college, or school to perform nontechnical or nonprofessional duties under the supervision of the professional staff; sometimes working voluntarily but usually paid on an hourly basis.

Student's Card. 1. In a public library, a borrower's card for the use of students, granting special privileges. 2. In some public libraries, a borrower's card issued for a limited period to out-of-town students attending school or college in the town.

Study. 1. A small room devoted to study. 2. A monographic publication presenting the results of an individual's research in a particular limited field, often issued by a university as a number of a serial publication.

Stylus, Electric. *See* Electric Stylus.

Subbranch. A small branch open fewer hours than the central library and the regular branches and giving only partial branch service.

Subdivision. 1. One of the parts into which a main class or a subordinate class is divided in a classification scheme. 2. One of the immediate smaller parts into which a part called a division is separated in a classification scheme. 3. A restrictive term added to limit a subject heading, *e.g.,* History, or Periodicals; or a term added for further limitation.

Subhead. A second, or a later, part of a subject heading, added to divide the entries under a subject; also, a second part of an author heading for a corporate body, as the name of a department or bureau following the name of a country or state.

Subject Analytic. An entry in a catalog under subject of a part of a work or of some article contained in a collection (volume of essays, serial, etc.), including a reference to the publication which contains the article or work entered. Also known as Subject Analytic Card, Subject Analytical, and Subject Analytical Entry.

Subject Authority Card. *See* Authority Card.

Subject Authority File. *See* Authority List or File.

Subject Bibliography. A list of material about a given subject, whether the subject be a person, place, or thing.

Subject Card. A catalog card bearing a subject entry.

Subject Catalog. A catalog consisting of subject entries only.

Subject Cataloging. That phase of the process of cataloging which concerns itself with the subject matter of books, hence, includes classification and the determination of subject headings.

Subject Classification. A classification scheme developed by James Duff Brown from his *Adjustable Classification*, in which only one place is assigned to a subject.

Subject Cross Reference. *See* Subject Reference.

Subject Departmentalization. The administrative division of the books in a large public library into several distinct units according to subject, as Civics and Sociology Department, Industry and Science Department, etc.

Subject Entry. An entry in a catalog or a bibliography under a heading that indicates the subject.

Subject Focus. *See* Subject Interest or Focus.

Subject Fulness. *See* Secondary Fulness.

Subject Heading. A word or a group of words indicating a subject under which all material dealing with the same theme is entered in a catalog or a bibliography, or is arranged in a file.

Subject Interest or Focus. The center of the special librarian's attention in subject fields; *i.e.,* the primary field of interest of the organization with which the library is connected, subjects logically related to the primary field but of secondary importance, subjects representing the work of departments and divisions of the organization, subjects relating to the administration of the organization, and subjects of common interest to libraries of the same general type, such as museum libraries, bank libraries, etc.

Subject Interests. Topics that appeal to readers, especially to those of the same age, sex, occupational, income, or cultural group.

Subject Library. *See* Special Library.

Subject Reference. A reference from one subject heading to another. Also called Subject Cross Reference.

Subject Series. A number of books, ordinarily not reprints, dealing with different phases of a single subject or with a special field of literature, usually by different individual authors, uniform in textual and physical characteristics and published by a single publisher. [Reprinted from Haines, *Living with books,* by permission of Columbia University Press.]

Subject Style. The use of red ink or black capitals in subject headings in a card catalog.

Subprofessional Assistant. A person who performs under the supervision of professional staff members work largely concerned with the higher routine processes peculiar to library work and requiring some knowledge of library procedure.

Subscription Book. A book for which a definite market is created, before or after publication, by soliciting individual orders.

Subscription Library. A library owned or controlled by an association composed of persons who acquire membership by the payment of annual dues or subscriptions.

Subsidiaries. *See* Reference Matter.

Substandard Film. Film the width of which is less than 35 mm., usually 16 mm. or 8 mm. [M.]

Subtitle. The explanatory part of the title following the main title; *e.g., The creative adult; self-education in the art of living.* [C.]

Summer Card. *See* Vacation Card.

Summer Reading Club. *See* Reading Club (2); Vacation Reading Club.

Sunday School Library. A collection of reading material owned and administered by a church school for the use of its students and teachers. Formerly, a collection of children's books maintained by a Sunday school.

Sunk Bands. In binding, cords or bands laid in grooves sawed across the backs of sections, designed to prevent ridges and to produce a smooth back. Distinguished from Raised Bands. Also called Sunk Cords.

Sunk Cords. *See* Sunk Bands.

"Super." *See* Crash (1).

Supercalendered Paper. Paper given a high gloss or polish by the pressure of supercalender rolls.

Superintendent of Documents Classification. *See* Documents Office Classification.

Supervisor. A staff member who directs the work of a given department or of a group of individuals, or who coordinates the work of related agencies doing special types of library work, as, supervisor of branches, supervisor of children's work.

Supplement. 1. A complementary part of a book or article, which adds information to or continues the original; usually issued separately. 2. An extra sheet, section, or number accompanying the regular issue of a periodical or a newspaper.

Supplementary Reading. Reading matter assigned for pupils to read in addition to textbook material. Also called Supplemental Reading, Supplementary Reading Sets, Supplementary Sets.

Supplementary Source. *See* Outside Source.

Supposed Author. An author to whom is attributed, by some authoritative source, the authorship of a book published anonymously or of doubtful authorship.

Suppressed. Withheld or withdrawn from publication or circulation by action of author, publisher, governmental or ecclesiastical authority, or court decision. Of a leaf, canceled from a book because of some imperfection or objectionable feature.

Surface Paper. *See* Coated Paper.

Survey. A scientifically conducted study through which data is gathered according to a definite schedule, which is presented in statistical, tabulated, or summarized form.

Swash Letter. An early italic capital having tails and flourishes. Also, any letter, though usually a capital, elaborated with flourishes.

Swivel Head. A projection head of a reading machine arranged to rotate around the projection axis so as to accommodate film with the image in various positions. [M.]

Syllabic Writing. Writing in which each character represents a syllable rather than a single sound.

Syndetic. Having entries connected by cross references; said of a catalog.

Synopsis. An orderly summary of the important points of a work, arranged for rapid consultation.

Systematic Catalog. *See* Classed Catalog.

Tab (Binding). A device for indexing and quick reference; usually a small piece of paper, card, or fabric attached to the outer edge of a page.

Table. A representation of any sort of information, in parallel columns or rows. To be distinguished from text in tabular form. [C.]

Table Book. An ancient writing book, consisting of wax-covered tablets of wood, ivory, or metal fastened to-

gether at the back by rings or thongs of leather, on which writing was done with a stylus.

Table of Contents. A list of preliminary sections, chapter titles, and other parts of a book, or of articles in a periodical, with references to pages on which they begin. Also called Contents.

Tablet. A piece of clay, or a thin piece of wood or other material covered with wax, on which in ancient times records were written.

Tail. 1. The bottom portion of a page. 2. By extension, the bottom portion of the backbone of a bound book.

Tailband. A former name for a headband at the tail of a book.

Tailpiece. A small ornamental design at the end of a chapter or at the bottom of a printed page.

Talking Book. A book recorded on phonograph records, which, because of the large amount of material on each record, must be played on a machine equipped with a slowly revolving turntable. Also known as Sound-recorded Book. The talking book was devised especially for the blind.

Talking Book Machine. A machine similar to a phonograph, manufactured especially for playing talking book records. It is electrically driven or spring driven, and is equipped with a slowly revolving turntable.

Tall Copy. A choice copy with wide

margins, printed on large sheets of paper little trimmed in binding. The term came into use in describing copies of early printed books when the margins of different copies of an edition varied with the size of the sheets of paper used.

Tapes. Pieces of tape, or strips of cloth, to which signatures are sewed and whose free ends are pasted to the boards, or inserted between the split boards, of the book covers to lend strength to the binding. *Cf.* Bands and Cords.

Teacher-librarian. A person trained to give service both as a teacher and as a librarian, whose position requires part-time service in each field.

Teacher's Card. A special borrower's card for teachers, giving certain extended privileges to meet their professional needs.

Technology Department. 1. The part of a library where a collection of books and other materials on technical subjects is kept for reference, study, and reading. Sometimes called Technology Division. 2. The administrative unit in charge of a technology collection and its use.

Technology Librarian. 1. A librarian in charge of the work of a technology department. For a department having a staff of two or more the terms Chief of Technology Department and Chief Technology Librarian are coming into use and are to be preferred. *Cf.* Chief. 2. A professional assistant in a technology department, as senior technology librarian.

Telescope Box. *See* Double Slipcase.

Text. 1. The author's work in a book, as distinguished from notes, commentaries, etc. 2. One of the versions of an author's work which may have been published with variations in different editions. 3. The main body of matter on a printed or written page, as distinguished from notes, etc. [Def. 3. By permission; from Webster's *New International Dictionary*, Second Edition, copyright, 1934, 1939, by G. & C. Merriam Co.] 4. The type matter of a page, as distinguished from the illustrations and margins. 5. The main part of a book, as distinguished from preliminaries, appendix, index, etc. 6. A term sometimes applied to black letter or Gothic type.

Text Title. *See* Caption Title.

Textbook Edition. An edition published for the use of students.

Thesis. *See* Dissertation, Academic.

"Third" Indention. The distance from the left edge of a catalog card at which, according to predetermined rules, certain parts of the description begin or continue; generally as far to the right of the second indention as the second indention is to the right of the first indention. [Ca.]

Three-color Process. *See* Process Color Printing.

Three Dots. *See* Marks of Omission.

Three-quarter Binding. Binding similar to half binding, except that the leather extends further on the sides, theoretically to three-quarters of half the width of the sides, and corners are proportionately large.

Three-quarter Leather. *See* Three-quarter Binding.

Throw. *See* Projection Distance. [M.]

Throwout. A leaf bearing a map, table, diagram, or similar material, mounted at the end of a volume on a guard the full size of the leaf, so that the leaf, when opened out, may be consulted easily as the book is read.

Thumb Index. A group of rounded notches cut out along the fore edge of a book, with or without tabs set in, on which are printed or stamped letters, words, or other characters showing the arrangement. Also called Cut-in Index and Gouge Index.

Tickler System. A method of recording or filing notes or material which should be followed up at a definite future date, such as unfilled requests, or forthcoming publications.

Tier. A vertical series of shelves between two shelf supports, commonly seven in number: one section of a press. Also called Section.

Ties. Cords, ribbons, or narrow strips of leather, attached to the edges of book covers or cases, designed to hold the front and back covers together.

Tight Back. The back of a book in which the covering material has been glued to the back. Confined mostly to leather-backed books.

Tight Joint. *See* Closed Joint.

Tilted Shelves. *See* Sloping Shelves.

Tilted-tab Guide. *See* Angle-top or Angle-tab Guide.

Time Number. *See* Biscoe Time Number; Merrill Book Number.

Time Record. A record of books charged that shows what books are due on a given day.

Time Stamp. A device, often an electrical device, for indicating time on various records.

Tip In. To paste a leaf, or leaves, on a printed sheet or into a bound book, without guards.

Tip-on. A leaf that has been tipped in on another leaf.

Title. 1. In the broad sense, the distinguishing name of any written production as given on the title page, including the name of the author, editor, translator, the edition, etc., but excluding the imprint. 2. In the narrow sense, the title does not include the name of the author, editor, etc. [C.]

Title-a-line. Having entries that occupy only a single line of type. Also known as One-line.

Title Analytic. An entry in a catalog under title for a part of a work or of some article contained in a collection (volume of essays, serial, etc.) including a reference to the publication which contains the article or work entered. Also known as Title Analytical Card, Title Analytical, and Title Analytical Entry.

Title Caption. *See* Incipit.

Title Card. A catalog card bearing an added entry under title.

Title Catalog. A catalog consisting of title entries only.

Title Edition. An edition distinguished from another edition of the same book only by a change on the title page, usually a change of date.

Title Entry. The record of a work in a catalog or a bibliography under the title, generally beginning with the first word not an article. In a card catalog a title entry may be a main entry or an added entry. [Ca.]

Title Indention. *See* "Second" Indention.

Title Leaf. *See* Title Page.

Title Letter. *See* Work Mark.

Title Mark. *See* Work Mark.

Title Page. A page at the beginning* of a book or work, bearing its full title and usually, though not necessarily, the author's (editor's, etc.) name and the imprint. The leaf bearing the title page is commonly called the "title page" although properly called also the "title leaf." [C.]

Title Page Date. The imprint date.

Title Reference. A reference in a catalog from a title, as from a title of a classic to author entries for the work.

---

* In the case of works in Oriental languages, the title page and the beginning of the text are normally at the back of the volume.

Title Sheet. The first signature of a book, containing title page, dedication, and other preliminary matter. Also called Title Signature.

Title Signature. *See* Title Sheet.

Title Vignette. *See* Vignette (2).

Tome. A volume; a book; particularly, a heavy volume.

Tooling. 1. Impressing an ornamental design on a book cover by means of heated "tools" (dies). Also known as Hand Tooling. 2. The effect thus produced.

Top Edge Gilt. *See* Gilt Top.

Topographic Map. A map that shows physical and cultural features of an area.

Township Library. A free public library maintained by a township.

Tracing. In a card catalog, the record on the main entry card of all the additional headings under which the work is represented in the catalog. Also, the record on a main entry card or on an authority card of all the related references made. The tracing may be on the face or on the back of the card, or on an accompanying card. [Ca.]

Tract. 1. A pamphlet made from a single sheet imposed in pages. 2. A pamphlet containing a short discourse, particularly one on a religious or a political topic, issued to serve as propaganda.

Trade Bibliography. 1. A list of books in print or for sale, compiled by a publisher, a bookseller, or a group of such agencies. 2. Collectively, the mass of such bibliographies.

Trade Binding. The binding on a trade edition.

Trade Book. A book published for sale to the general public through the bookselling trade, as distinguished from a textbook, a subscription book, or a book meant for a limited public because of its high price, technical nature, or specialized appeal.

Trade Catalog. 1. A book or pamphlet issued by a manufacturer or a dealer, or by a group of manufacturers, illustrating and describing their products or goods and sometimes including, or accompanied by, a price list. 2. A trade bibliography. Also called Trade List.

Trade Edition. The edition of a book regularly printed and supplied by the publisher to booksellers, as distinguished from a textbook edition or a limited edition of the same book.

Trade Journal or Paper. A periodical devoted to the interests of a trade or industry and its allied fields.

Trade List. *See* Trade Catalog (2).

Trade Literature. Catalogs and other advertising or promotional material distributed by business firms, usually free of charge.

Trade Paper. *See* Trade Journal or Paper.

Trade Series. *See* Publisher's Series.

Trailer Strip. A piece of blank film attached to the hub end of a reel to protect the last frames and to facilitate threading the film on the spool. [M.]

Trained Assistant. An assistant who has received professional education in a library school.

Training Class. A program of systematic training for library service which emphasizes practical work and is conducted by a library primarily for members of its own staff. Distinguished from apprentice class by its more formal and extensive instruction.

Transactions. 1. The published papers and abstracts of papers presented at a meeting of a learned society. 2. Proceedings (*q.v.*).

A general distinction sometimes made between Transactions and Proceedings is that Transactions are the papers and addresses and Proceedings are the record of the meeting.

Transcript. A copy, usually written or typewritten, made from an original; particularly, a copy of a legal document.

Transfer. Changing the registration of a borrower from one agency of a library system to another; especially, from a children's department to an intermediate department or to the general library.

Translator. One who renders from one language into another, or from an older form of a language into the modern form, more or less closely following the original. [C.]

Transliteration. A representation of

the characters of one alphabet by those of another. [C.]

Translucent Screen. A light-diffusing material on which a projected image is viewed by transmitted light. [M.]

Transmitted Light. Light that has passed through a transparent or a translucent material. [M.]

Traveling Card. A duplicate main entry catalog card recording holdings for a serial, filed in an official serial catalog or some other official file until additions to the record are made, when it replaces the corresponding card in a public catalog until the next addition.

Traveling Library. A small collection of selected books sent by a central library agency for the use of a branch, group, or community during a limited period.

Traveling Library Department. The administrative unit of a library or library commission that selects and distributes traveling libraries.

Traveling Men's Library. One of a group of subscription libraries at one time placed in hotels for the use of traveling men, who could borrow books at one hotel and exchange them at another hotel participating in the plan. *Obsolete.*

Tray, Book. *See* Book Tray.

Tray, Card. *See* Card Tray.

Treasure Room. A room, or part of a reading room or a stack, where rare and particularly valuable material is housed. Also known as Rare Book Room.

Tree Calf. Calf that has been treated so as to produce a design resembling the trunk and branches of a tree.

Trial Proof. *See* Proof (2).

Trim. To cut the edge of a leaf, or a group of leaves, of a book.

Trimmed Edges. Book edges that have been cut to make them smooth.

Trimmed Flush. *See* Cut Flush.

Triple-entry Charging System. A method of recording book loans in which three records are kept: a time record, a book record, and a borrowers' record.

Triptych. An ancient hinged writing tablet consisting of three tables of wood, metal, or ivory, covered with wax on the inside surfaces, on which writing was done with a stylus.

Truck. *See* Book Truck; Inventory Truck.

Trustees, Board of. *See* Board of Trustees.

Turkey Morocco. Originally, a morocco derived from goatskins that came from Turkey. Now widely imitated by the use of goatskin finished with a fine hard grain or a bold cross grain.

Turn-in. The portion of a book cover formed by folding in the overlapping material on the three edges.

Twelvemo. *See* Duodecimo.

Two Along. In bookbinding, a method of sewing on bands, tapes, or cords that treats two adjoining sections as a single unit, a method generally used for thick volumes composed of thin sections, to avoid making the bound volume too thick at the back. Also known as Two On and Two Sheets On.

Two-card System. 1. A charging plan based on the issue of two borrower's cards to a patron, one of them for the charging of restricted material. 2. A double-entry charging system (*q.v.*).

Two On. *See* Two along.

Two Sheets On. *See* Two along.

Two-way Paging. The system of page numbering used for a book with texts in two languages, one of which reads from left to right (English, etc.) and the other from right to left (Arabic, Hebrew, etc.), when the texts are in two distinct sections with page sequence from opposite ends to the center of the book. [Ca.]

Type. 1. A rectangular block, usually of metal or wood, having its face so shaped as to produce, in printing, a letter, figure, or other character. 2. Such blocks, or the letters or characters impressed, collectively. [By permission; from Webster's *New International Dictionary*, Second Edition, copyright, 1934, 1939, by G. & C. Merriam Co.]

Type I Library School. A school for education in librarianship accredited by the Board of Education for Librarianship of the American Library Association, which is part of a degree-conferring institution, requires at least a bachelor's degree for admission to the first full academic year of library science, and/or gives advanced professional training beyond the first year.

Type II Library School. A school for education in librarianship accredited by the Board of Education for Librarianship of the American Library Association, which is part of a degree-conferring institution, requires for admission four years of appropriate college work, and gives only the first full academic year of library science.

Type III Library School. A school for education in librarianship accredited by the Board of Education of the American Library Association, which is part of a degree-conferring institution, or of a library or other institution approved by the Board for giving professional instruction, does not require four years of college work for admission, and gives only the first full academic year of library science.

Type Face. 1. The printing surface on the upper end of type that bears the letter or character to be printed. 2. The character, or the style of the character, on a type.

Type-facsimile. A reprint (properly a page-for-page and line-for-line reprint) in which the type and general appearance of the original are imitated as closely as possible. [C.]

Type Ornament. *See* Floret (1).

Type Page. The printed portion of a page.

Type Size. The measure of the dimensions of type, taken from the body rather than from the face. Formerly designated by name, now more commonly, by points. *See also* table in appendix.

Typescript. A copy of a work in typewritten form, as distinguished from one in printed or handwritten form.

Ultra-violet Light. Light that has a wave length shorter than that of visible violet light. [M.]

Unauthorized Edition. An edition issued without the consent of the author or the representative to whom he may have delegated his rights and privileges.

Unbound. Without leaves or signatures fastened together, as a periodical volume ready for binding or not yet complete.

Uncial. A large rounded letter in early writing, a modification of the capital.

Uncut. The edges of the book not cut smooth by the binder's machine. [C.]

Unexpurgated Edition. *See* Expurgated Edition.

Unfinished Book. A book of which a part was published but the rest was never completed or published.

Uniform Title. The distinctive title by which a work which has appeared under varying titles and in various versions is most generally known. Also called Conventional Title. [Ca.]

Union Catalog. 1. An author or a subject catalog of all the books, or a selection of books, in a group of libraries, covering books in all fields, or limited by subject or type of material; generally established by cooperative effort. Also called Repertory Catalog and, sometimes, if on cards, Card Repertory. 2. A Library of Congress depository catalog combined with cards issued by other libraries, including sometimes cards prepared by the library having the depository catalog. Sometimes called Union Depository Catalog. 3. A central catalog (*q.v.*).

Union Depository Catalog. *See* Union Catalog (2).

Union Finding List. *See* Union List; Finding List.

Union List. A complete record of the holdings for a given group of libraries of material of a given type, in a certain field, or on a particular subject. Sometimes known as Union Finding List.

Union Shelf List. *See* Central Shelf List (2).

Union Trade Catalog. *See* Consolidated or Union Trade Catalog.

Unit Card. A basic catalog card, in the form of a main entry, which when duplicated may be used as a unit for all other entries for that work in the catalog by the addition of the appropriate heading. Library of Congress printed cards are the most commonly used unit cards. [C.]

Universal Decimal Classification. *See* Classification Décimale Universelle.

University Library. 1. A library, or a system of libraries, established and maintained by a university to meet the needs of its students and faculty. 2. The central library of such a system.

Unopened. The folded edges of an uncut book not divided by hand for reading. Such a book might be "opened" but still be "uncut." [C.]

Unpaged. Numbering omitted from pages.

Unrecorded Book. A book found to exist though nowhere recorded, as a newly discovered book, a book merely surmised to exist, or one considered lost.

Untouched. Not rubricated or illuminated.

Untrimmed. The folded edges (bolts) of the book uncut, and the uneven edges of the projecting leaves not pruned square by the cutting machine. [C.]

Upper-case Letters. Capital letters of a font, so called from their position in an old-style case for type.

Upright Stroke. *See* Line Division Mark.

V Slip. A formerly used small slip, 5 x 7.5 centimeters.

Vacation Card. A special borrower's card issued for a vacation period, allowing extended privileges. Some-times called Summer Card or Summer Loan Card.

Vacation Charge. The loan record of a book on which an extended circulation period has been allowed during vacation.

Vacation Club. *See* Vacation Reading Club.

Vacation Reading Club. A group of readers organized by a library to follow a more or less flexible program of recreational reading during the summer. Also called Summer Reading Club and Vacation Club.

Variant. *See* Issue (Edition, etc.).

Variant Copy. *See* Issue (Edition, etc.).

Variorum Edition or Variorum. 1. An edition that contains notes of several editors and commentators. From the Latin *Cum notis variorum*. 2. An edition of a publication containing variant readings, or versions, of the text. [Def. 2. By permission: from Webster's *New International Dictionary*, Second Edition, copyright, 1934, 1939, by G. & C. Merriam Co.]

Vellum. 1. A thin sheet of specially prepared calfskin, lambskin, kidskin, or pigskin. 2. Originally, a thin calf gut or lamb gut, specially prepared for use as parchment, for writing or for bookbinding.

Vellum Finish. The natural, smooth, unembossed finish of book cloth.

Version. 1. A translation; often used for a translation of the Bible. 2. One of the forms in which a legend, romance, fairy tale, etc., is presented.

Verso. The left-hand page in an open book, usually bearing the even page number. Also, the back of a separate printed sheet. Formerly called "folio verso." *Cf.* Recto. [C.]

Vertical File. 1. A case of drawers in which material may be filed vertically. 2. A collection of pamphlets, clippings, and similar material arranged for ready reference upright in a drawer, box, or suitable case.

Viewer. *See* Hand Viewer. [M.]

Vignette. 1. In manuscripts, an ornamental design of vine tendrils decorating an initial. 2. An engraving, or other picture, without a definite border and with its edges shading off gradually. Loosely, any ornamental design before a title page, on a title page, or at the beginning or the end of a chapter. A vignette on a title page is called a Title Vignette.

Viscose Film. Film that is rendered photosensitive by impregnation with a light-sensitive dye. [M.]

Visible Cloth Joint. A cloth book joint so made that the cloth can be seen in the finished book.

Visible File. *See* Visible Index (1).

Visible Index. 1. A series of metal frames or panels for holding card records so that a group of cards can be seen at one time. Also called Visible File. 2. A record kept in such a device, as a list of serials, with or without holdings.

Visitor's Card. A temporary borrower's card issued to a transient borrower.

Visual Aids. *See* Audio-visual Materials.

Vocal Score. *See* Piano-vocal Score.

Volume. 1. In the bibliographical sense, a book distinguished from other books or from other major divisions of the same work by having its own inclusive* title page, half title, cover title, or portfolio title, and usually independent pagination, foliation, or register. This major bibliographical unit may have been designated "part" by the publisher, or it may include various title pages or paginations. . . . 2. In the material sense, all that is contained in one binding, or portfolio, etc., whether it be as originally issued or as bound** after issue. The volume as a material unit may not coincide with the volume as a bibliographical unit. When a physical unit designated "part" by the publisher is too large or too extensive to be bound with one or more others, it is called a volume in collation, but in contents and notes the publisher's designation is followed. [Ca.] 3. For library statistical purposes, any printed, typewritten, mimeographed, or processed work, bound or unbound, which has been cataloged and fully prepared for use. In con-

---

* In cataloging, the most general title page or half title, or the cover title, is the determining factor in deciding what constitutes the volume; *e.g.,* a reissue in one binding, of a work previously issued in two or more volumes, is considered one bibliographical volume.
** Such a composite volume bound by or for the individual owner may contain either two or more bibliographical volumes of the same work, or two or more works published independently.

nection with circulation, the term volume applies to a pamphlet or a periodical as well as to a book.

Volume Number. 1. A number assigned to a volume of a serial, a set, or a series. 2. A number added to a book number to distinguish one volume from another volume of the same work.

Volume or Part Signature. The number of the volume, or a letter indicating its sequence (as "a," "b," etc.) given on the same line as the signature, but toward the inner margin of the first leaf of a gathering.

Voluntary Reading. *See* Free Reading.

Waiting List. 1. A want list (*q.v.*). 2. A list of patrons who are to be notified when a certain book is available.

Waiting List Books. 1. Books listed in a want list. 2. Books which the library has been requested to hold for patrons when the books are available.

Wall Shelving. Bookcases placed against a wall.

Wallet Edge. The edge of a limp-leather binding in which the back cover is extended to overlap the front edge of the volume, terminating in a tongue to be inserted through slots in the front cover when the book is closed.

Want File. *See* Want List (1).

Want List. 1. A file recording books and other material which are to be purchased when funds are available,

prices have been reduced, or publications are available. Also known as Waiting List, Want File, Possible Purchase File, Desiderata. 2. A list of books or other material that a library wishes to acquire by exchange.

War Service Library. One of the libraries sponsored by the American Library Association under the direction of the War Service Library Committee, for the use of the American armed forces during the first world war.

Wash Bath. A water bath used in development to wash off the developer before the film goes into the fixing bath, or a water bath in which the film is washed after it leaves the fixing bath to remove the hypo in the film. [M.]

Wash Drawing. In book illustration, often a black and white drawing done with a brush.

Waste Papers. The halves of the fly leaf* sheets which in some types of binding are cut away, or pasted down, one over the other, on the inner face of the cover before the board paper is fastened to it. [C.]

Watermark. Semitransparent letters, figures, or an emblem, seen in paper when it is held to the light; produced in the process of manufacture. Sometimes called Papermark.

Weeding. The practice of discarding or transferring to storage superfluous copies, rarely used books, and material no longer of use.

_____

*Definition 1.

Weekly. A periodical issued once a week.

Whipstitching. *See* Overcasting.

White Line. A method of wood engraving in which engraved lines appear in the print as white against a black background, indicating tones and colors.

White Paper. A popular name derived from its white cover for: 1. A document issued daily to members of the British Parliament, containing the parts of the Blue Paper of the preceding day that relate to the business of the day. 2. A document issued by the British government stating its policy or proposals regarding a subject.

Whole Binding. *See* Full Binding.

Whole Number. The number assigned by a publisher to an issue of a periodical or other serial counting from beginning of the publication, in distinction from numbers assigned for volume and number or for series and volume.

Who's Who File. *See* Biography or Who's Who File.

Wire Binding. Any form of binding in which the leaves are held together by wire. Formerly restricted to wire-stitched pamphlets; now applied to various forms of spiral or coil binding.

Wire Line. One of the close parallel lines that appear in handmade paper when it is held to the light; produced in the process of manufacture.

Wire Stitching. Stitching a pamphlet or a magazine with wire staples, either side-fashion (side stitching) or saddle-fashion (saddle stitching).

Withdrawal. The process of removing from library records all entries for a book no longer in the library.

Withdrawal Record. A record of all books officially removed from a library collection.

Wood Block. 1. A block of wood on which a design for printing has been cut in relief. 2. A print from such a design.

Wood Engraving. 1. The process of engraving a design in relief on hard wood, generally boxwood, cut across the grain, with a graver or burin, and printing impressions from it. The work may be done so as to produce black lines, or white lines for the rendering of color, or both black and white lines. 2. A print made in this way.

Wood Pulp. A pulp made from wood, used in the manufacture of newsprint and cheap book paper.

Wood-pulp Magazine. *See* Pulp Magazine.

Woodcut. 1. A method of cutting a design in relief on a wood block along the grain with knives and gouges (not with a burin or graver as in wood engraving), and printing impressions from it, the parts left standing printing black and the parts cut away appearing as white in the print. 2. A print from a wood block cut in this way.

Word-by-word Alphabetizing or Alphabeting. Arranging alphabetically, with words rather than letters as units.

Work Manual. *See* Procedure Manual.

Work Mark. The part of a book number that distinguishes one title from other titles by the same author when the books have the same class number. Sometimes called Title Mark or Title Letter.

Work Room. A room in which any of the technical and manual processes are carried on.

Work Slip. *See* Process Slip.

Work Space (Stack). That part of a stack allotted to assistants for routine work, including necessary space for card cabinets, book trucks, etc. It is an element included in calculation of floor areas and cubic feet of stack.

Worm-bore. A hole or a series of holes through a book, made by a bookworm. A book in this condition is said to be "wormed."

Wove Paper. Paper without wire marks. Distinguished from Laid Paper.

Wrap-case. A threefold wraparound protective case for precious books, usually provided with guards for the top and bottom edges.

Wrapper. 1. An original paper binding. 2. A book jacket (*q.v.*).

Wrong Font. In proofreading, a type of wrong size or face appearing improperly in matter composed from type of another font.

Xylographic Book. *See* Block Book.

Yapp. *See* Divinity Circuit.

Yearbook. 1. An annual volume of current information in descriptive and/or statistical form, sometimes limited to a special field. 2. One of a series of annual reports of cases judged in early English law courts.

Yellowback. A popular, cheap novel; —so called from the former practice, especially in England, of binding such books in yellow board or paper covers. [By permission; from Webster's *New International Dictionary*, Second Edition, copyright, 1934, 1939, by G. & C. Merriam Co.]

Young People's Department. A section of a library for the use of older boys and girls and young adults. Sometimes called Intermediate Department.

Zinc Etching. 1. A photomechanical process of producing a line engraving through the medium of a metal plate, usually of zinc, etched in relief by acid. 2. An engraving thus produced. Also called Line Etching, Zincograph, and Zinco.

Zinco. *See* Zinc Etching (2).

Zincograph. *See* Zinc Etching (2).

APPENDIX I

BOOK SIZES

FOLD SYMBOL	NAME	SIZE LETTER	APPROXIMATE SIZE IN INCHES	OUTSIDE HEIGHT IN CENTIMETERS
64 mo. or 64°	Sexagesimo-quarto	Sf	2 by 3	to 7.5
48 mo. or 48°	Quadragesimo-octavo	Fe	2½ by 4	7.5 to 10
32 mo. or 32°	Tricesimo-secundo	Tt	3½ by 5½	10 to 12.5
18 mo. or 18°	Octodecimo	T	4 by 6½	12.5 to 15
16 mo. or 16°	Sextodecimo	S	4 by 6¾	15 to 17.5
12 mo. or 12°	Duodecimo	D	5 by 7⅜	17.5 to 20
12 mo. (large)	Duodecimo		5½ by 7½	
8 vo. or 8°	Crown Octavo	O	5⅜ by 8	20 to 25
8 vo. or 8°	Octavo		6 by 9	
8 vo. or 8°	Medium Octavo		6⅛ by 9¼	
8 vo. or 8°	Royal Octavo		6½ by 10	
8 vo. or 8°	Super Octavo		7 by 11	
8 vo. or 8°	Imperial Octavo	Q	8¼ by 11½	
4 to. or 4°	Quarto	F	9½ by 12	25 to 30
fo. or f°	Folio		12 by 19	from 30 centimeters

Book sizes in French are designated in the following manner: in-folio (in-fol.); in-quarto (in-4° or in-4); in-octavo (in-8° or in-8), etc.

APPENDIX 2

TYPE SIZES

		FORMER NAME	EXAMPLES OF TYPE FACE
5 point em quad	■	Pearl	in Old Style
6 point "	■	Nonpareil	in Old Style
7 point "	■	Minton	in Old Style
8 point "	■	Brevier	in Old Style
9 point "	■	Bourgeois	in Old Style
10 point "	■	Long Primer	in Old Style
11 point "	■	Small Pica	in Old Style
12 point "	■	Pica	in Old Style
14 point "	■	English	in Old Style
18 point "	■	Great Primer	in Old Style

APPENDIX 3

A SELECT LIST OF ABBREVIATIONS

Based on those encountered by readers who examined library literature in search of terms for the glossary.

a.	année (year), aus (from).
A.	Auflage (edition), Ausgabe (edition).
a.l.	autographed letter.
A.L.A.	American Library Association.
a.l.s.	autographed letter signed.
Abdr.	Abdruck, -drücke (copy, impression).
abr.	abridged, abridgment.
Abt., Abth.	Abteilung, Abtheilung (section, part).
add.	additional.
adm.	administration.
all pub.	all that has been published.
an., anal.	analytic, analytical.
Anm.	Anmerkung (note, annotation).
ann.*	annals.
anon.	anonym, anonymous.
annot.	annotated, annotator.
ap., app.*, appx., apx.	appended, appendix.
arr.	arranged, arrangement.
as., asst.	assistant.
Aufl.	Auflage (edition).
aug.*, augm.*	augmented.
Ausg.	Ausgabe (edition).
auth.	author.
auth. an.	author analytic.
b.	born.
B.	Band (volume), Buch (book), Beitrag (contribution).
bd.*	bound.
Bd(e).	Band (Bände) (volume).
bearb.*, Bearb.	bearbeitet (edited), Bearbeiter (editor).
Beil.	Beilage (addition, enclosure, supplement).
bi-m.	bimonthly.

* The same abbreviation may be used for the corresponding word in another language when the abbreviation commonly used in that language has the same spelling, *e.g.*, augm. for augmentée.

bi-w.	biweekly.
bib., bibl., bibliog.	bibliography.
bio-bibl.	biobibliography.
biog.	biography.
bk.	book.
br.	branch.
bul., bull.	bulletin.
c.	circa (about), copyright, command paper.
C.B.I.	Cumulative Book Index.
ca.	circa (about).
cat., catlg., catal.	catalog, cataloger, cataloging.
cd.	command paper.
cf.	confer (compare).
ch.	chapter, children.
chap.	chapter.
chron.	chronological.
cl., clo.	cloth.
cm.	centimeter.
cmd.	command paper.
col.	collector, colored, column.
comp.*	compiled, compiler, complete.
Cong.	Congress.
cont.	containing, contents, continued, contemporary (e.g., cont. bdg.—for contemporary binding).
cop.	copy.
cor.*, corr.	corrected.
cr. (fol., 4° or 4to, 8° or 8vo, etc.).	crown (folio, quarto, octavo, etc.).
cyc.	cyclopedia.
d.	died.
D., D°	duodecimo (twelvemo, from 17½ to 20 centimeters).
D.C.	Decimal Classification, Dewey Classification.
D.D.C.	Dewey Decimal Classification.
dept.	department.
diagr.	diagram.
diss.	dissertation.
doc.	document.
dmy.	demy.
dup., dupl.	duplicate.
E.C.	Expansive Classification.
e.g.	exempli gratia (for example).
ea.	each.

ed.*, edit.	edited, edition, editor.
Einl., Einleitg., Einltg.	Einleitung (Introduction).
encyc.	encyclopedia.
eng., engr.	engraved, engraver, engraving.
enl. (ed.)	enlarged (edition).
engr. t.-p.	engraved title page.
erg., Erg.	ergänzt (supplemented), Ergänzungsheft (supplement).
f.	folio (sheet).
F., F°.	Folio (30 centimeters and over).
f.n.	footnote.
fac., facsim.	facsimile.
fasc.	fascicle.
Fe.	quadragesimo-octavo (from 7½ to 10 centimeters).
ff.	folios (leaves), following.
fict.	fiction.
fig.	figure.
fl.	flourished.
fo., fol., fol°.	folio.
fold.	folded, folding.
fold. pl.	folded (folding) plate.
front.	frontispiece.
g.	gilt.
g.e.	gilt edge.
g.t.	gilt top.
g.t.e.	gilt top edge.
G.P.O.	Government Printing Office.
ges., gesam.	gesammelt (collected).
Govt. print. off.	Government printing office.
gr.	great.
gt.	great.
H.M.S.O.	His (Her) Majesty's Stationery office.
H.M.Stationery off.	His (Her) Majesty's Stationery office.
hb.	half-bound.
hds., hdschr.	handschrift (manuscript).
hf.cf., hf.cl., hf.lea., hf.mor.	half calf, half cloth, half leather, half morocco.
hft.*	heft (number, part, stitched book).
hrsg., Hrsg.	herausgegeben (edited), Herausgeber (editor).
hsgb., Hsgbr.	herausgegeben (edited), Herausgeber (editor).

i.e.   id est (that is).
il., illus.   illustrated, illustration, illustrator.
illum.   illuminated.
imp.   imperfect, imported, improved.
impr.*   imprimerie (printing establishment).
in-(in-f., in-fol., in-4, in-4°,
  in-8., in-8°.)   in-folio, in-quarto, in-octavo.
inaug-diss.   inaugural-dissertation.
inc.   incomplete.
incl.   included, including, inclusive.
incompl.   incomplete.
incr.   increased.
introd.   introduction, introductory.

j.   journal.
J.   Jahr (year)
Jahrh., Jh., Jhr.   Jahrhundert (century).
jnl.   journal.
jour., jourl.   journal.
juv.   juvenile.

k., kgl.   königlich (royal).

l., ll.   leaf, leaves.
L.C.   Library of Congress.
lea.   leather.
lf.   leaf.
Lfg., Lfrg.   Lieferung (number or issue of a periodical or
                                       serial).
lib.   library.
libn.   librarian.
Lief.   Lieferung (number or issue of a periodical or
                                       serial).
livr.   livraison (fascicle).
ln.   librarian.
ltd.   limited.

mem.   memoir.
misc.   miscellaneous.
misc. doc.   miscellaneous document.
mim.   mimeographed.
mm.   millimeter.
mo.   monthly.
ms., mss., MS., MSS.   manuscript, -s.

n.d.   no date of publication.
n.f.* (n.F.)   neue Folge (new series).

n.p.	no place of publication.
n.pag.	nicht paginiert (unpaged).
n.s.*	new series.
n.t.-p.	no title page.
nar.	narrow.
new ed., rev., and enl.	new edition, revised, and enlarged.
new ser.	new series.
no.*, nos.	number, -s.
nouv. éd.	nouvelle édition (new edition).
numb.	numbered
O.	octavo (from 20 to 25 centimeters).
o.J.	ohne Jahr (without date of publication).
o.O.	ohne Ort (without place of publication).
o.p.	out of print.
ob., obl.	oblong.
p.*	page.
p.l.	preliminary leaf.
pa.	paper.
pam.	pamphlet.
pap.	paper.
per., period.	periodical.
phot., photos.	photograph, -s
pl.	plate.
pm.	pamphlet.
por., port., ports.	portrait, -s.
pp.	pages.
pph.	pamphlet.
pref.	preface, prefixed.
prel.ll.	preliminary leaves.
prelim., -s.	preliminary matter, preliminaries.
priv.pr., priv.print.	privately printed.
proc.	proceedings.
ps., pseud.	pseudonym.
pt., pts.	part, -s.
ptie.	partie (part).
pub.*	published, publisher.
pubd.	published.
publ.	publication.
Q.	quarto (from 25 to 30 centimeters).
q.v.	quod vide (which see).
r., rect., r°.	recto.
ref.	reference.

rept.	report.
rev.*	reviewed, revised.
rpt.	report.
russ.	russia (leather).

S.	Seite (page), sixteenmo (from 15 to 17½ centimeters).
s.a.*	sine anno (without date of publication).
s.l.*	sine loco (without place).
S.T.C.	Short Title Catalog.
sd.	sewed.
ser., sér.	series, série (series).
Sf.	sexagesimo-quarto (up to 7½ centimeters).
sh.	sheep.
sig.	signature.
Sm. (fol., 4to, 8vo).	small (folio, quarto, octavo).
subj.	subject.
subj. an.	subject analytic.
sup., suppl.*	supplement.

t.*	title, tome, tomo.
T.	octodecimo (from 12½ to 15 centimeters).
t. (th.).	teil (theil) (part, section, volume).
t. an.	title analytic.
t.e.g.	top edge gilt.
t.-p.	title page.
tab.	table.
tr.*, trans.	translated, translator, translation.
trans.	transactions.
Tt.	tricesimo-secundo (from 10 to 12½ centimeters).
typ.	typographie (printing office).

übers., uebers.	übersetzt, uebersetzt (translated).
umgearb.	umgearbeitet (revised).
unb., unbd.	unbound.
unct.	uncut.
unp.	unpaged.

v.	verso.
v., vol.	volume.
v.d.	various dates.
v.p.	various paging, various places of publication.
vel.	vellum.
verb.	verbesserte (corrected).
Verf.	Verfasser (author).

verm.	vermehrte (enlarged).
vo.	Verso.
wdcts.	woodcuts.
wh.no.	whole number.
wk.	week.
y., yr.	year.
Zg., Zt., Ztg.	Zeitung (newspaper).